FINDING
PEACE,
ONE PIECE
AT A TIME

WHAT TO DO WITH YOUR AND A LOVED ONE'S PERSONAL POSSESSIONS

© 2019 Rachel Kodanaz

Library of Congress Cataloging-in-Publication Data
Is available from the Library of Congress.

Printed in the United States of America.
0 9 8 7 6 5 4 3 2 1

Fulcrum Publishing
4690 Table Mountain Drive, Suite 100
Golden, Colorado 80403
800-992-2908 • 303-277-1623
fulcrum.bookstore.ipgbook.com

RACHEL KODANAZ

FINDING PEACE, ONE PIECE AT A TIME

WHAT TO DO WITH YOUR AND A LOVED ONE'S PERSONAL POSSESSIONS

FULCRUM

Finding balance between logical and emotional thinking is a constant battle that we all face. As a beneficiary of some logical thinking in the face of unspeakable hardship, I am immensely grateful for the memories and objects that have survived since my father's passing. When we think about the need to take care of ourselves in tragic moments, thinking of our future selves and families is just as important. As I continue to thank my mother, you will also find yourself giving self-thanks on many occasions.

With love and encouragement from
Rachel's daughter, Gretchen Blythe Kodanaz

CONTENTS

PREFACE

I can't remember whether I ever embraced material things
as a child, or if I had a longing to connect either with
my own possessions or those of my ancestors. Yes, I did
treasure my bicycle, but not as a possession – as a mode
of transportation. I wasn't someone who collected music,
girly things, or even clothing. My art projects came home
from school but were not saved. My swim-team medals
and ribbons went in a box, never to be opened. I have
very few pictures of my childhood, as taking and sharing
photographs were not what they are today. As a tomboy,
I was satisfied playing stickball, swinging from monkey
bars, or playing field games rather than collecting possessions. Growing up in a less-than-model household led me
to value and rely on independence over material things.

When I left home for college, I packed all my possessions accumulated over the years into my car and brought
them to my dorm room. The inventory was simple: clothing, a few books, my record albums, a turntable, and a
few miscellaneous items with emotional value such as my
high school yearbook, address book, and a few mementos
from friends.

Never to return to my childhood home again, I
continued to carry with me my minimal possessions. Of

course, as I entered the "real world" with a "real job" I began collecting furniture, tchotchkes, and what would someday become my prized possessions. I viewed these items as an extension of my physical being; I didn't have emotional relationships with them. They were, at the time, mostly necessities.

As the years went on, the addition of my husband, Rod, and our baby expanded the collection of personal and family belongings, and it began to take on more emotional value. We took more family pictures, kept trinkets of our daughter's birth and the curl from her first haircut, and collected other childhood memories. I still remained a minimalist, favoring experience over items of convenience, such as constructing a makeshift bed while traveling instead of bringing a portable crib, or calculating a trip to the park versus a backyard swing set. My husband and I both had well-paying jobs, so my rationality for not purchasing these items was not due to economics but rather to keep from collecting what I didn't need. I will admit that when our corporate jobs moved us cross-country, we hired a moving van rather than loading our precious possessions in the backs of our cars. While my possession count increased, I still maintained that my relationships with them were strictly due to their utilitarian value, not my emotional connection to them. These were our things, and while I had my favorites, they did not hold an overly sentimental value to me. At least that's what I thought at that time.

All that changed one day in April when I experienced the sudden death of my husband.

Our day started like every other day, with our morning routine of getting ready for work, preparing our lunches, filling our daughter's diaper bag, and walking into the garage for the last time as a family. Rod clicked our daughter's seatbelt in her car seat, and we kissed each other good-bye and both drove off to work.

In literally a heartbeat, my world changed. The phone rang. It was that fateful call from the vice president of the company where Rod and I worked. Rod had passed; he suffered from arrhythmia and was gone in seconds. When reality found its way to my heart, I realized he was never physically coming back to our house. I painfully learned that his possessions, and even mine, had a new meaning. They told both Rod's life story as well as our story together. The items held the physical presence of our shared memories, experiences, growth, connection, and time we had together. These memories became the link to "us," preserving each breath we took as a couple and a family. All the possessions he touched became my sacred items. These precious items created a special bond, allowing me to feel him right by my side – a new form of physical touching.

Until Rod's passing, I viewed my personal possessions as a means to support my existence. They were physical necessities to create comfort, feel a sense of security, and provide a sanctuary or a safe haven in which my little family could live. I won't deny that I found pleasure in having and surrounding myself with nice things, living in an up-and-coming neighborhood, dining at hip restaurants, tackling new sports, and driving reliable cars. But

I was oblivious to the real meaning of possessions until Rod passed away. Following his death, every square inch of my home provided a cherished memory, every piece of clothing became "remember when," and every personal item of his became mine to figure out what to do with. Was I supposed to keep everything? Was I supposed to give his stuff to his parents, as he preceded them in death? What do I save for our daughter? Why did he save what he saved? So many questions, so many choices, so many unknowns, so few answers. I felt like I was a ball in a pinball machine with everyone around me telling me what I should and should not do with his belongings. They spoke as if they were the experts, informing me what the appropriate timing was following his death to clear out his personal belongings from our house and what to do with them. They even went so far as to tell me I could never get over his loss if I didn't box up his belongings. *Really?* What was there to get over? My husband was dead; my daughter was fatherless. Besides, how would they know? I just tuned them all out.

If, in this case, we define *possession* as owning and keeping something of meaning or interest, something that holds memories for its owner, then for me, the lasting impression of Rod's belongings were permanently tattooed on my heart and mind. Suddenly, each and every item of Rod's had meaning, and if I didn't know the meaning of the object, I was determined to find out where it came from and why he kept it. I now owned all his keepsakes from his childhood until his death, and these keepsakes told a beautiful story of a very special man.

As I sorted, obsessed over, and cherished each of his things, the story of Rod unfolded with great meaning. While it was a difficult, complicated, and heart-wrenching process, I found myself in a warm, safe place, with just the two of us reconnecting in a very special way. I realized all of his items represented him, and now I looked at them through a different lens. Maybe it was because I had no other choice, or maybe it was because I felt him right next to me. Either way, I learned his possessions told a story of his life, and I was signed up to read, write, and share his legacy with family, friends, and future generations.

In writing *Finding Peace, One Piece at a Time*, my desire is to share my experience of what I have learned through Rod's passing, and to support friends, family, clients, and readers in understanding the impact of *their* possessions. The expression "If I only knew then what I know now" might be considered a cliché, but that's how I feel when I refer to my personal belongings. If I could do it over again, I most likely would have saved more of "me" to share with my second husband, Taner; my daughter; and my future grandchildren. I regret that I chose not to save my collection of childhood swim awards, the colorful ribbons, each with a small white cardboard form stapled to the back to record official race times, race information, and team members. At the time, I remember cherishing the recognition, as I was a proficient swimmer and very proud of my accomplishments. My daughter began swimming at the age of five in a sport that had not changed in the thirty years since I had raced; the length of the pool as well as the individual and relay races remained the same. As she collected her own ribbons, creating memorabilia books of her successes, I truly felt the sadness and loss of not having my ribbons to share with her to compare our accomplishments. If only I had kept the items, had known that one day they would be important to me.

Rod passed at a very young age, and while I was largely alone in widowhood among my peers back then, I have since experienced the inevitable passing of other loved ones and have watched friends lose parents and grandparents as we've continued to age. And through all of these experiences, one of the questions I am often asked is what to do with the possessions. This usually leads to the question about time frame. Some of us have the luxury of time, while others have legal or economic constraints that force the grieving process to move too quickly. Despite the good intentions of my family and friends to sort through Rod's belongings quickly, I was not forced to move, which allowed me to work through my own process in my own time. But what about other families and partners who are not so fortunate? How do we make the right decisions now and leave ourselves time to revisit certain pieces? Does it all have to happen at once? I'll answer that one now. No, of course not. And as we ourselves age or think about our own legacies, what do we want our families to have and cherish?

In the pages that follow, my hope is to provide you with an understanding of possessions, our relationship with these items, and the importance they have in our lives and the lives of our loved ones. Consider the pages to be a guide in helping you understand the importance of what has influenced you through your interaction with people, your physical and emotional relationship with possessions, and the impact they have on *your story*. Once you have a better understanding of your relationship to your and your loved ones' possessions, you'll be stronger and better equipped to make decisions about them when the time comes. This book will help you explore different life transitions that involve making decisions about possessions, including after a death, when downsizing a home, and when preparing your home and possessions for your own passing. In addition, the guidance you'll find in these pages will help your own day-to-day life be simpler and less encumbered, creating space for the current and next chapters in your life.

The words and interpretations found in this book are meant to plants seeds, which can blossom when you are ready to start the process of sorting, thinning, and redistributing your or a loved one's personal possessions.

– *Rachel Kodanaz*

CHAPTER 1

THE MEANING OF POSSESSIONS

DEFINITION OF POSSESSIONS

Until Rod's passing, I was unaware of the true significance of a personal possession – something belonging just to you, something that doesn't have meaning to anyone but you. The night I learned of Rod's death, I returned home from the hospital to the house we shared as a family. The realization that he was never coming home took my breath away and sent shivers up my spine. In a rage of anger, I grabbed his toothbrush and threw it violently across the room. I was so angry that he had passed, leaving me with such uncertainty. Of course, his untimely death was not his fault. As I sat on the bathroom floor crying, staring at his toothbrush, my mind drifted to the thought, *What do I do with his toothbrush?*

From that moment forward, everything I touched of his personal possessions, from his socks to his family heirlooms, now became mine. Someday I would have to figure out what to do with everything, but for now, his T-shirt became my pajamas, his briefcase quickly became my daily work bag, and his coffee mug was my morning companion. While I immediately repurposed some of his belongings, the rest would have to wait until I was ready – which could be never.

What I didn't learn in school, or through my family experiences, or in my short thirty-one years was what happens to a loved one's belongings when they die. Do you keep these items forever? Are they boxed and placed in the attic? Do you give stuff away? Logically I knew that someday I would need to sort through his drawers, finding a new home for his belongings, but emotionally I was unaware of how one could possibly embrace this endeavor. If I didn't do it, who would? It would have to be me; I would never allow anyone else to touch his things. Nothing he owned belonged in the trash – not even his toothbrush.

The first lesson Rod's belongings taught me was that items have both physical and emotional attributes – what we see and what we feel. I needed to embrace the notion that his shirts were more than something he wore to work, his running shoes were more than just a pair of shoes, and his eyeglasses were more than something to help his vision. All of his belongings represented his life, and I wanted to savor the stories and memories each one held for myself, our daughter, friends, and family members.

My challenge was that I didn't know what to do next. I just wanted to spend time with Rod's possessions, as they were his things and I wanted to be with him. As

I learned about the meaning of possessions, I discovered how intertwined we are with our things and how much comfort they can provide. Who knew his red coat could have provided such warmth and security?

The most notable insight to come out of Rod's death was that our personal possessions tell a unique story that should be captured, embraced, shared, and cherished forever. Of course, these belongings do not replace a person; they do, however, provide a tremendous amount of comfort, connection, and reassurance.

IMPRESSIONS OF POSSESSIONS: WHAT YOU SEE

Throughout our entire life we collect, rearrange, give away, purchase, downsize, thin, repurpose, and throw away items that were once of interest to us, including clothing, books, school papers, furniture, and electronics. Some of us have a tendency to collect more than others, some of us save more than others, and some of us are very quick to tidy up and part with our possessions. In most cases, our decisions about what to keep are hastily made in the moment without regard to future consideration and reflection.

Regardless of where you or a family member fall on the possession-management spectrum, the items collected – whether physical or digital – are considered personal belongings that have value and meaning for their owner. We begin collecting and saving items at a very early age, documenting our lives by tucking them away in our drawers, under our beds, and in boxes. These items provide a snapshot in time signifying likes, hobbies, connections, proudest moments, and our most vivid memories. Collectively they, along with our life experiences, write our personal story to keep for ourselves or share with future generations.

As a parent, watching my daughter figure out the importance of her belongings provided me with the opportunity to watch the early stages of her formulating her personal story. She was very involved in sports, the arts, music, reading, and her stuffed "siblings," therefore each item she added to her "save" box was well thought out. I often pondered when the time came for her to revisit these items if she would remember why she chose to save specific artwork, a particular friendship bracelet, or a memento from one of her sports team. What I did know was that these items were part of her text, and she was taking the lead on writing her manuscript, piece by piece. To this day, I wonder how much I influenced her decisions based on what I had learned from my experience with Rod's passing: that our possessions – physically, digitally and emotionally – tell a compelling story, one worth preserving.

During my daughter's school years, we developed a system for collecting and saving her keepsakes. Our technique included four large, plastic storage containers, each displaying a label – one each for elementary school, middle school, high school, and college. As each box filled up, she had to decide what to discard if she wanted to add more. Occasionally when she asked for my opinion, I provided input, otherwise I truly enjoyed being a bystander, simply observing her decisions. The process made it clear to me that she had a distinct vision of which items to save, items that for her conjured an emotional reaction representing a time and place. Sometimes she saved a Playbill from a Broadway show, other times she didn't. Sometimes she saved notes from friends, other times they went into the trash. As an onlooker, I saw how each choice was clearly based on the experience or impact a particular item represented. Strangely, in her middle school box she saved the purple cast removed from her arm after healing from a snowboarding accident. I remember at the time trying to figure out why she would want to save such an odd object, and one that took up substantial space in her box. I could only speculate that it was to reminisce about a traumatic childhood experience, perhaps to represent the timing of her transition from skiing to snowboarding, or maybe she thought it was a cool item to show her children. The why doesn't always matter.

In their physical state alone, our possessions may not carry much obvious significance; it's the relationships we develop in their presence, through their function or while obtaining them, that create the lasting connection. My husband, Taner, is Turkish, and his extended family still largely resides in Turkey. His parents moved from Turkey to America twice, once for a dozen years during which Taner and his older brother were born, and then again in a permanent capacity when he started middle school. He shared with me the story of his stressful move from the United States back to his homeland of Turkey when he was just six years old. As part of the move, he packed his clothing and toys to be shipped in containers to Ankara. His possessions included an American football, a banana seat bicycle, his Tonka truck, and his Matchbox car collection. These were his keepsakes, the most current and relevant possessions he had accumulated as a kid. Upon his apprehensive arrival in Turkey, he was surprised to find instant fame. He became the coolest kid on the block, as his things were unique and truly foreign to his new friends. His belongings transformed from his toys to his lifeline, allowing him to feel important, welcomed by his peers, and certainly making for an easier transition to a new country with very different customs and culture. During his time in America, these objects were pure entertainment. They were fun to have, but all the neighborhood kids had them too. Now they became something more: a novelty, an instant friend-maker, a comfort zone in the new unknown.

The significance and importance of our possessions may transform as we enter adulthood. With maturity, our tastes develop and grow, and so do the objects we choose to embrace. While Taner would inevitably outgrow his bike and American football, our house is now full of Turkish tea sets, mirrors, and rugs inherited from his extended family. When friends and new acquaintances come to our home and marvel at the beautiful dressing robe, salvaged rice sacks, or authentic headpieces on display, he gets immeasurable joy reminiscing about his beloved grandmother who was a cornerstone of his years in Turkey. As I watched my daughter toss certain mementos from friends and keep others, I thought perhaps the ones she kept made her laugh, while others had simply lost significance. And as we grow and move, our lifestyles may prompt our purchases. For example, someone living in Florida may accumulate beach chairs, water toys, and a boat, while a person from Colorado might accumulate ski equipment, warm clothing, and other mountain gear. As I grew up on the beaches of Connecticut and Rhode Island, I would not have believed it if you told me I would later spend the majority of my adult life in landlocked states away from an ocean. It just wouldn't sound possible. Now my skis and mountain bike give me far more joy than my beach towel. (Although, I do still strive to get my toes in the sand at least once a year.) To me, the evolution is both fascinating and deeply rewarding. How wonderful to say that throughout my life, I have experienced the beach life of New England, the farmlands of Kansas and Iowa, and the high-altitude adventuring of Colorado. How wonderful that Taner's time in Turkey as a young child has contributed to a lifelong appreciation of diversity, travel, and delicious food. Most importantly, with those experiences we have collected possessions that tell our story.

To me, our elaborate world of electronic devices has created a new complexity in defining possessions. How do these square and rectangular gadgets fit into "our story"? The machines collect an incredible amount of data that was once physical in nature: photos, documents, contact information, to-do lists, books, music, credit cards, maps, and an assortment of applications to store and manage our data. Our personal electronic devices are meant to be used by one person; therefore, what we save on the device is unique to each of us. There was a time when my medical records were in a file cabinet; now they are stored electronically along with my fitness log, contacts, birthday list, and the rest of my personal information. The transition from physical to digital possessions may eliminate boxes of physical items such as photographs, address books, medical records, and legal documents, but the digital form is just as important as the physical – it just takes up less space. Our relationship with these items remains the same regardless of their format, as many of the items in our "stored" boxes can be scanned and shared electronically. For some, the transition to electronics allows for your possessions to literally be at your fingertips.

Whether our prized objects come in physical or digital form, they represent items you can see and sometimes touch. They are things that can be passed down to future generations. I'll admit now that in the twenty-five years since Rod has passed, the quantity of his physical possessions has decreased. But the ones that remain still carry enormous significance, perhaps even more in their scarcity. Despite the numerous technological advancements in both size and efficiency, it was so heartwarming to hand over to my daughter some of the camping gear that Rod and I used on our honeymoon. And I know it was fun for her too. Even though some of the kitchen equipment probably wouldn't even work anymore, using the same bowls and mugs while out in the woods with her new family was a special opportunity to include Rod in her life. These things that we choose to keep are our idio-syncratic mark on our personal history. Similarly, photos of our grandparents in their youth are always a bit of a shock – they look so different from how we have known them. But to be able to look into their youthful and optimistic eyes, you can probably see a bit of yourself – either physically or emotionally. They too faced the same firsts, the same apprehensions, the same ambitions, and the same fears. As we lose and gain family, these possessions have the power to transcend time and place and are continuously able to conjure a connection much greater than simply being a thing to look at or hold.

EXPRESSIONS OF POSSESSIONS: WHAT YOU FEEL

Our belongings can embody an array of emotional responses, including happiness, sadness, growth, change, pleasure, grief, sorrow, joy, and even anger. Some might even say our essence lives on in what we currently and once owned. As our possessions become more infused with our emotions, they create lasting memories, becoming extensions of who we want to be and where we want to belong. And as our lives unfold, our things symbolize our sense of self-identity, becoming "receptacles" for our emotions and memories.

Recently, a widowed friend asked for my support and expertise sorting through her husband's personal belongings. I suggested we start in the garage, the part of the house that can facilitate a feeling of accomplishment with fewer emotional ties. Instead, she wanted to start in the master bedroom closet. She felt that clearing, sorting, and discarding some of the items there could provide a real sense of progress, as this was an area of the house she frequented. Even though a closet can be an emotional place to start, she felt strong enough to tackle the project with my help. The walk-in closet was large, his belongings on the right, hers on the left. We decided to start with his shoes, as he owned many pairs of sneakers, and she felt clearing them would open up space for us to move around a bit more easily. Once we successfully sifted and boxed her husband's shoes, she quickly began rearranging the closet by moving her shoes over to the shelves we had recently cleared. I followed her lead, sorting her boxes of shoes and placing them on the empty shelves. Just when I felt we had found our rhythm, I turned around to find her on the floor crying. Her tears were triggered by memories of times she had worn each pair with her husband. She was flooded with memories of where they had gone, what they had done, and whom they had celebrated. In this case, it was her own belongings that had conjured the feelings of sadness; she would never again be able to wear her favorite heels or sandals on an evening with her husband.

Watching my friend, I was reminded of my most vivid memory of truly feeling the emotional connection to my shared belongings, one that occurred within weeks of Rod's death. Once my friends and family had returned to their own personal routines, I found myself walking around in circles in my own home. I experienced bouts of sporadic crying and struggled to determine the trigger. I soon realized my once-cherished family photographs were the culprit. In the shock and newness of it all, seeing Rod's smiling face sparked pain and anxiety rather than fond memories. In my quest to find tranquility, I simply turned the frames on their sides for a few months to help alleviate my adverse reaction to the memories. In time, I was able to right the photos and find joy in the recollections and cherish his smiling face.

My friend and I both experienced triggers over relatively small objects, but what about the bigger pieces? What about a car, for example? This is a prized possession that can show both financial responsibility and a sense of independence. It is also functional, freeing, something to be proud of, and something we can't save forever. We can, however, save the emotional connection it provided through pictures, stories, and memories. When thinking of the car, we can recall the early days of freedom the car may have provided, allowing us to come and go as we pleased and the wonderful feeling of a sense of responsibility. The stories and memories experienced with the car may conjure great memories, establishing a true connection. When my daughter was in elementary school, my husband, Taner, purchased a large SUV to help me with carpooling to swim-team practice, trips to the mountains to ski, and for me to feel safe. While I always felt that the SUV was too big, I cherished the memories that particular vehicle provided me with: priceless hours of "windshield time" with my daughter and her friends, allowing me to listen to endless stories of their daily lives.

As they sat in the backseat chit-chatting I soaked up the day's latest drama and learned about her friends. To this day, when I see an old SUV similar to the one I owned, I immediately think of the special days in ours – a memorable possession steeped with emotional connections.

Why else would we save a corsage from prom? Not for the beauty, as they don't maintain the original look or feel, but instead to savor the special feeling we experienced when the flower became ours. Our possessions often personify the affectionate memory they represent. A coffee mug is a useful tool to drink hot liquids, but our favorite coffee mug is determined by the pleasure it provides based on its physical characteristics or the emotional connection we have to it. One of my friends started a tradition with her father: every morning after pouring her coffee in her favorite mug she sent her dad a photo of herself with it to say good morning. A special way to start her day, the physical coffee mug, one of her prized possessions, provided a wonderful connection to another person.

Sometimes we collect possessions simply for their beauty, items that provide pleasure merely by looking at them rather than by interacting with them. For many people, just looking at a piece of art provides warmth, a sense of relaxation, and a welcomed distraction. My mother collected Hummel figurines, which are small, porcelain figurines. She was incredibly proud of her collection, and she found pleasure displaying the figurines in a glass case in the corner of the living room, the part of the house that was off-limits to the grandbabies. These fragile porcelain pieces of art brought her great pride, as they represented the notion of worth, value, and beauty. Those who are true art collectors may value their collections in similar ways. While they are physical in nature, their beauty provides a different relationship.

A wedding ring conveys beauty, personal significance, and an emotional association to a special person. A ring alone in a jewelry store might have a distinct style and beautiful diamond, but it has no meaning other than it might represent a pending engagement or marriage. However, when the ring is yours, it represents a very different story. In my case, when I look at my left finger I see the connection to my family, my husband, and my daughter, who helped pick out the ring when we all became a new family. Glancing at my wedding ring conjures an emotional reaction, as the ring shouts *you are loved* – truly one of my most emotionally prized possessions.

I am often asked if I consider consumables to be possessions. Why not? Often smells or tastes create priceless memories. If a bottle of perfume is considered to be a physical possession, isn't the huge wave of positive emotion you get when you walk by someone wearing your late mother's perfume an emotional reaction to a possession? The same is true for tastes. I only have to have one foot out of a cab in New York City to have my taste buds salivate over the impending bite of a famed NYC bagel. The taste and texture create not only a connection to a possession but also to a childhood memory.

As with consumables, the relationships we share with people and pets might be considered a form of possession, drawing a meaningful comparison between our emotional connection to possessions and how we cherish relationships – how we embrace them, honor them, and show gratitude for them.

Similar to physical possession, people and pets may enter your life for a period of time and through life's transitions or death. And while they may not be physically present, your emotional connection will always be there, captured by experiences shared. The associations, memories, and experiences are part of remembrances and are forever connected to your heart.

Evolution of Possessions: How They Transform

In the days of the Vikings and Egyptian kings and queens, personal possessions were buried along with the body. Many historians believe these burial practices were based on the belief that a person would need the same food, furniture, and animals to live peacefully and for eternity in the afterlife. In modern times, however, rather than burying a person's prized possessions we instead bestow them to the next generation of family and friends, allowing the new guardian an opportunity to embrace a connection and transform an object's value, significance, and possibly even function. As life and loss force us to evolve, there is certainly a clear distinction between those things that we immortalize and want to treat with extra care, such as a museum object that should rarely be touched, and those whose physical touch on a daily basis provide strength, love, encouragement, or whatever support it is you need. As with a child and their teddy bear, proximity and physical touch can make a difference. While a furniture piece can provide solace to an entire family, sometimes it is a thoughtful transformation of a once everyday object that can have a lasting impact on a person or family's well-being and overall grief journey.

If you look around your house, you might see repurposed items from family members. Your grandmother's candy dish that once housed your favorite treats might become a knickknack on your bookshelf alongside your grandfather's old smoking pipe. Your kids might balk at the pipe, wondering what such an odd-shaped thing actually does; however, the memories of him smoking the pipe while sipping his scotch on the rocks and watching TV is your reality. My grandmother had a curio display cabinet filled with china and a variety of other precious trinkets. She was so attached to this piece that it moved with her from Connecticut to Florida and then back north to New Jersey. When the time came that she could no longer live on her own, her new living arrangements were sadly too small for her cherished cabinet. One of my sisters recognized the importance this piece had to our grandmother and felt a similar connection to it – it was steadfastly present every time we visited her homes. To my grandmother's delight, my sister kept the piece, modernizing it slightly, and it still has a place in her home to showcase her own family's treasures. As for the rest of us, the cabinet brings back warm memories when we see it at holiday dinners.

Several years ago, while presenting at the Tragedy Assistant Program for Military Survivors (TAPS) conference, a woman walked by the podium with a beautiful tote bag. The colors, size, and design of the bag were what caught my attention, and as I looked closer, I saw a name embroidered into the cloth. We struck up a conversation about the bag, and I learned that after her son had passed away in combat, she refashioned his fatigues into a bag that she could proudly use every day. She shared that her son's uniforms had been stored in a closet for years as she pondered a way to repurpose them in a way that would both honor his military career and create a forever connection to him. She was proud of his accomplishments, his service, and now her bag, which showcased his medals and prominently displayed his name. It was the perfect memorial for all to see. And the greatest gift from repurposing his belongings was the number of complete strangers asking questions about her son, just as I had. It is truly a special recognition and a great transformation for a uniform that would have otherwise remained in a box in the top of a closet.

In a similar case, a fellow widow shared with me pictures of a few quilts she had made for her two young children using her husband's clothing. Having lost her spouse when her twins were only eighteen months old, she was desperate to make sure the legacy of their father was alive and well as they grew up. I felt for her, as one of my biggest sadness triggers was the realization that my daughter was too young to remember Rod. As the woman described the quilts, I was struck by the beautiful story they told; each square represented a different part of her husband's life – his childhood, marriage, the birth of the twins, and his illness. As the girls grew up, what a powerful connection to know that their father was right there alongside them on movie night.

On a recent trip, my daughter and I took to see Rod's father, my father-in-law walked us around the house sharing stories of his life as he always does. But this time felt different. Since the passing of his wife, he had started to reminisce on their nearly seventy-year marriage and to contemplate his own age and imminent passing. Knowing that his time in this house, where he had lived all these years with a loving wife and had raised six kids, fourteen grandkids, and now a new generation of great grandkids, was coming slowly to an end, he began opening his boxes of saved possessions. Inside were track signs he had made fifty years ago when he was track coach, old tools, coin collections, and wooden toys. We had been visiting his house for more than thirty-five years looking at the same photos he cherished from his time in the US Navy and the same blown-glass bowls in the cupboard, yet this particular afternoon was particularly memorable. As a father who had lost a son, he typically shared small findings from Rod's childhood, such as an old report card or a wooden soapbox car model, yet on that afternoon he included more about himself and my late mother-in-law. It was a pleasure to have a more holistic view of the family in which Rod grew up and for my daughter to learn even more about the early life of her grandparents.

A common ritual among widows is to wear their husband's wedding ring on their thumb or around their neck as a constant reminder of their life together. Like my peers, I did the same. I felt a warmth in my heart when I would look down at my hand and see Rod's ring. I remember the day we purchased it, the day I slid it on his finger, and the day the hospital nurse handed it to me when he passed. Such joy and sorrow in one little circle. While I found comfort with his ring on my thumb, I always feared I would lose the precious keepsake as it was still a bit too big. On a brave emotional day, I decided to make a trip to the jeweler who had designed the braided metal band and requested his assistance in resizing the ring to fit my finger. The jeweler was hesitant as he believed cutting and resizing the ring would leave a blemish where the excess metal was removed. I convinced him that the ring would have no meaning sitting in a drawer, but wearing it on my finger would always keep me connected to Rod. As weird as it may sound, I was truly content in having the imperfection, as I was reminded daily that Rod's ring had evolved to become my personal possession – a forever remembrance of him. As we said on our wedding day, the ring was a sign of our love, and I wanted to stay true to that vow, blemish or not.

For many partners in particular, our loved ones' possessions have a unique meaning. They are the reminder of a life partnership that started with vows of eternal hope, optimism, and boundless possibility for the future. It is rare that a couple sharing their vows at the end of the aisle know that "till death do us part" is closer than not. But, unfortunately, our worst fears can come true at any time. Many fortunate widows do, however, find a second chance at love. What to do, then, when old love meets new love? I struggled with this question when Taner first came into my life. I was still living in the same house Rod and I had bought, and there were many reminders of him. While Rod was no surprise to Taner, it was still a bit of an awkward transition as he moved into my house. As a new husband who was incredibly patient, supportive, and respectful of my widowhood, we needed to figure out a way to blend our newly expanded family that left room for Rod's memory and significant place in our family, while also working to find a unique path forward as a family of three again. Oftentimes it comes down to finding a shared meaning for those possessions that we have chosen to cherish. A client's husband was a handyman around the house, and he loved to collect tools and other items for home improvement projects. His workbench and storage drawers were perfectly organized and well labeled. He was incredibly proud of his collection and it showed. Following his sudden death, my client found tranquility spending time rummaging through his workbench, looking for the perfect screw or tool that she needed while abiding by his organization and labeling. She chose to leave everything as he left it, which made her feel that she was working with her husband on her new projects. After remarrying years later, her new husband moved into her home, and they decided to keep the workbench rather than replace it. He instead added his own tools to the workbench and drawers. The new collection was truly a blending of his, hers, and theirs, and by merging together some physical possessions, they were able to add yet another layer of emotional connection between the past and future.

Our possessions will continue to transform in life and in death. As we continue to share these items with others for personal use, repurposing, or blending old meaning with new, the peace process will continue.

CHAPTER 2

FINDING PEACE

BEFORE WE CAN FIND PEACE

In order to find peace in parting ways with your or a loved one's personal belongings, you first need to *acknowledge* that a life transition has occurred. Whether you are downsizing a home, moving aging parents to assisted living, or cleaning the closets of a loved one who has passed, understanding the emotional implications of the transition is the first step. When we hear, "Mom, is it time for you to move?" or "Honey, should we downsize to a smaller house for financial reasons?" or "It's been awhile since Hannah passed, what should we do with her clothes?" those ideas need to be digested before an action can occur. Life's transitions are meaningful, emotional, stressful, and real regardless of when in life they occur. Owning, recognizing, and acknowledging that the transition is occurring allows us to take the next steps toward finding peace with saved and collected possessions – whether they are ours or a family member's.

After acknowledging a change has occurred, it's time to *face the fears* of the transition itself. This can mean changes to our lifestyle, our future, our relationships, our routines, our independence, our personal direction. One of these alone is overwhelming, so combining them is sure to create anxiety, resistance, and inner unrest. The most common source of anxiety is the fear of change, and going even deeper, the question becomes whether it's the actual change we fear or the fear of how the change occurs. Maybe the challenge is not about moving an aging parent but rather their understanding of how they will get from their home of fifty years to a new place. Who will pack up their belongings? Who will help them decide what to bring with them? What do they do with the stuff that won't fit? Isn't it easier to stay where they are? All of these are valid questions, but there are many solutions to these uncertainties if we are able to first face the fear. We must always remember that our personal story will remain the same, that the memories and connections to people and possessions are ours to keep. It's the future or the next chapter that is unknown and often scary. The fear of change can be conquered.

When I was a child, every Sunday morning we sat around my grandparents' dining room table. We indulged in my grandmother's egg casserole, sharing stories and experiences of the week. The time was so special, with my grandfather sitting proudly at the end of the table in his armchair as my grandmother created a warm and inviting atmosphere. Every week, I looked forward to our visits and our ritual. But, as with everything else, times changed, we grew up, my grandfather passed away, and my grandmother became too frail to live on her own. When the time came for her to move into an assisted-living home, I was overwhelmed with fear that our special routine that had fostered so many memories for me would end. My recollections with her were so vivid and wonderful that I wanted to be able to re-create those Sunday mornings with my own family. So, after my grandmother left her house, I moved the table, chairs, and side hutch to Colorado. And, although my grandmother passed before she met my family, her presence is felt and she is part of our story. Each holiday, as I sat around the table and looked down at the craftsmanship of the inlaid wood, I felt more at peace with her passing. The memories I was creating were both new and very much reminiscent of our weekly ritual. In my heart, I was relieved that the ritual had evolved rather than ended.

If the first challenge on the road to finding peace is to acknowledge the journey ahead, the next is to think about timing. Keep in mind, however, that in this case timing is amorphous. There are no set timelines or rules that will lead you straight to your peaceful place, only suggestions and ideas to help with the process of downsizing, rightsizing, or sharing belongings. If you were to survey a hundred people experiencing a life transition on the best time to start the sorting, thinning, and redistributing possessions, the results would show a hundred different responses. The timing is based on when *you* are ready or when there is an external prompt that requires attention. For example, you're looking for a financial document in the office, and the next thing you know you've shredded an entire drawer of papers that you hadn't been able to face until then. Or maybe you are forced to move due to circumstances out of your control, and it's finally time to face that closet that has remained closed since your loved one passed. These kinds of things may trigger you to react without thought; however, you *don't* have to decide on the spot what you want to keep or give away. Perhaps that one drawer was an inspired or liberating activity, but the next one is too much for today. Or maybe you are only able to make decisions about some of the things in that closet but not others. Even if your family members pack up your belongings to expedite a move, you can revisit the boxes at a later date. Just label the boxes and give yourself a pat on the back for whatever progress you were able to make. If the goal is to find peace, we need to take the action, but more importantly, we must give ourselves the time to find reconciliation with our things and what they mean to us.

A dear friend lost his battle with cancer several years ago. From diagnosis to death, only two short years passed before his variety of treatments and surgeries proved to be unsuccessful. In the final months of his life, his wife had tried to encourage him on his stronger days to take their five-year-old out to the shed and sort through his personal possessions: his sports equipment, camping gear, childhood keepsakes, handyman tools, car parts, garage paraphernalia, and some true junk. Her motivation was to help her husband share his belongings with his son before he passed. Although he would likely not remember the details, she wanted her son be able to hear the stories directly, connect with the possessions, and be close to his dad for as long as possible. The trouble was that my friend was having an incredibly hard time acknowledging his imminent death, and he couldn't emotionally handle the symbolic act his wife was encouraging, however beautiful it sounded. All three of them were on a journey to find peace with what was in the shed and what it represented; however, their timing was simply not in sync. I am not really sure if there is a solution or best practice if you are faced with a similar situation other than respecting each point of view. In this case, each family member had individual needs; however, the underlying truth was they didn't want the death to occur. In the years that followed my friend's death, Taner and I helped his wife sort, box, and save the most memorable possessions to pass on to her son. I was honored to walk with her in such a protective space, listening to the stories she shared with her son and watching his reaction.

Finding peace is further complicated when the possession is not a traditional physical item but instead something that might be more complex, less tangible. What if you're the last person in a family lineage to own and maintain a family business, but you have neither the interest nor the necessary resources to carry the torch any farther? Further, there may be an absence of heirs, resources may be thin, there may be no one with the necessary skill set(s), the market forecast could be bleak or markets might have shifted, or technology advances may have rendered the business obsolete. Any or all of these can mean a tough reality to face, one fraught with emotional challenges for those forced to make difficult decisions. The guilt alone can be overwhelming. For example, while I was working with a family member who had inherited an eighty-five-year-old family business with no written or legal provisions for its legacy, a daughter was torn over how to act. Her father had implied he wanted the business to remain in the family forever; however, he hadn't shared any specific thoughts on how that would be achieved. Following his sudden death, the daughter was torn between her family obligation to continue her father's dream and what was really best for her and the vision she had for her own future. Her internal struggle stemmed from the fact that she had never intended to take over the family business because she had never felt passionate about owning it. Yet in making her decision, she didn't want to disrespect her family's hard work. How do you honor the livelihood and successes of generations before you and make sure that you don't erase a beautiful history? Before making the decision to sell the business, the daughter decided to create a memory book celebrating the tradition of growing up with the family business that could be shared with future generations. In the end, she found peace with selling the business and applying the proceeds toward starting a business of her own that she felt in her heart her father would be proud of. In this case, she ultimately did fulfill her father's wishes – the nature of the business may have changed, but she succeeded in the tradition of self-run entrepreneurship.

Although many of us are not challenged with selling a family business, we may be faced with deciding, for example, what is best for our parents' or grandparents' china cabinet and all of its contents. In many of our families, our parents and their parents proudly displayed their china in their dining rooms as a symbol of a successful marriage, large family gatherings, and monetary wealth. In their minds, the china would be passed from generation to generation to be used at formal dinners and holidays. It was a sign of adulthood, and no part of the collection should be allowed on the children's table or in the dishwasher. I will admit, I have fond memories of holiday celebrations at my aunt's home where all the relatives brought their collection of china to combine for the evening. The table always looked beautiful, special, and festive. What happened to that tradition? Family dynamics have certainly changed. Now, we value the time-benefit of the dishwasher over the display-value of fine china. Our dining habits are increasingly relaxed, and children are typically present at the adult table. Further, the formal dining room has been replaced with open-concept living spaces, and our casual dinner sets are replaceable with a quick trip to the internet when an accident occurs. Unfortunately, for some aging parents, this is a difficult concept to understand; to them, china is not a thing of the past but rather an heirloom that should be passed from generation to generation. When faced with what to do with the china, the decision is truly in the hands of its new owner. In my opinion, honor their wishes by taking the boxes home, setting the table at least once with the china, and then figuring out how to find peace with it – whether keeping the box, donating it, or sharing it with someone else.

There is no question that collecting possessions is much easier than dispersing them to family, friends, and those in need; the fear of losing the connection to people, to the items themselves, and to the memories they hold is a valid reaction to the process. And as the new guardian of these objects, we are empowered to make decisions that are right for us. Remind yourself that the more difficult or complex the decision, the greater the fear, anxiety, and guilt will be. But you are not alone in your decisions. One search on eBay or Craigslist will confirm the reality that for most, fine china is a keepsake of the past. Sometimes, letting go is the only way we can find peace.

WHY IS FINDING PEACE IMPORTANT?

If we don't find peace, how will we heal? If we don't find peace, how will we ever let go of anything? If we don't find peace, how will we reconnect with the possessions we decide to keep? If we don't find peace, how will we share our or our loved one's story? If we don't find peace, how do we write the next chapter of our lives? If we don't find peace, how do we get over our fears? And if we don't find peace, how do we reconcile our guilt? Just like the answers to these questions, the importance of finding peace will be discovered over time. The process requires resolution, commitment, patience, and knowing that there are no mistakes, no wrongs. Sometimes we just might need to learn how to let go.

And when you do find the balance between what to keep and what to let go of, you will eventually find peace with your decision. There will likely be occasions when you regret or question a decision about a particular item. But don't we all occasionally wonder why we donated that sweater we miss? As you read the pages of this book, digesting the stories and ideas, you'll discover your own definition of peace, the ultimate certainty of resolving what to keep and what to discard.

Even when we're just dealing with our own possessions, parting with them can be scary. How can we add our favorite shirt to the donation pile if we have not yet accepted that the shirt's life has reached its end? Once a favorite, it now has a few holes, no longer fits properly, and is definitely out of style. It's time to accept that the shirt once held a very special place in the closet, and to acknowledge that the fond memories will not be forgotten. Nevertheless, it is time to find it a new home. While this is a simple and straightforward example, it is very real. I have learned both through my own experience and through helping friends that decluttering our own closets, without a significant life transition, can be a traumatic experience. How many times have you added something to a donation pile only to remove it and put it back in your closet? Regardless of the size, value, or purpose, anything that holds sentimental value requires that we first find peace before we can allow it to move on to its new home. Just like the example in Chapter 1 of the fond connection to a car, there comes a time when we are forced to allow the item to become our history, an earlier chapter in our story.

I have spent time with clients who have accumulated boxes and boxes of items in their basements for years, unaware even of what they contain. And yet they continue to accumulate without sorting, labeling, or thinning. Before long, they have created controlled chaos, perfectly piled boxes filled with mystery contents. If you were to ask why they continue to save the items, their answers will vary, but the foremost reason will be that they "just can't seem to let them go." No different from how we deal with items we inherit when a loved one has passed, we have to teach ourselves that letting go of our own possessions does not mean we are letting go of the associated love and memories. It's not that we are forgetting or that those memories or objects don't matter to us anymore, it's simply that our lives and homes must also allow and encourage space for the present and future.

Finding peace can also help us move past difficult roadblocks that are adversely affecting us. And, as an added benefit, our decisions could greatly benefit others. I had one client who was stubbornly attached to his collection of seven winter coats, yet he rarely went outside when the temperature was below forty degrees. When I asked him if the time had come to give away his coats, he said absolutely not. He harshly rejected my question, retorting that they were his coats and he had no intention of parting with them. I tried again by asking the question differently and was pleasantly surprised when I got a different response in return. In my new approach, I asked him how he felt about donating his coats to people experiencing homelessness, as the winter in his area was long and cold. After contemplating my proposition for a minute, he immediately went to the closet, removed six of his seven coats, and handed them to me. I had planted a seed. Initially he had responded defensively, and then when I provided a reasonable idea, he was able to find peace in parting ways with his coats, as he was now helping others who would benefit from his assistance. His belongings could revive their original purpose, and he found peace in knowing they weren't just being taken away or thrown out.

In another example, I was helping an older woman downsize from a two-bedroom independent-living apartment to a one-bedroom assisted-living arrangement. With her declining mobility, she was now using a walker on a daily basis. Our first task, then, was to set up her new closet in a manner that would allow her to comfortably access her clothing while still holding securely on to her walker. Sorting and thinning her clothing was easy, as she discarded items that were difficult to put on, didn't fit well, or didn't contain a pocket for her cell phone. We were moving along with relative speed until we got to her shoe collection. She resisted adding any of the shoes to the donation pile. Although she wouldn't articulate why, I felt certain that the reason she couldn't part with her shoes was that it meant acknowledging she could no longer wear them; some were now a bit too hard to walk in. For her, being forced to give up wearing favorite pairs of shoes only emphasized her age and all that came with it. They were beautiful, they were expensive, and they had life left in them, so I understood that parting with them had to be difficult. I could only imagine the memories that were flooding back of her younger years – years filled with parties, holidays, weddings, dancing, and other special occasions when she wore those beautiful shoes. They represented a time past, and for her, giving them away symbolized an official end to the life she had once been able to live. Yet she was simply not willing to let the shoes go, even though doing so was the most practical space-saving solution by pure volume. But when I asked if she had a friend or family member who would find pleasure in wearing the shoes, she perked up. She called her granddaughter who wore the same size shoe, and she was thrilled to be the new recipient. I helped my client box up the shoes, and we sent them to her granddaughter. Regardless of whether her granddaughter would have the same level of appreciation for the shoes, what mattered was that they found a special home.

Some people simply fear where their items might end up. I joked recently to a client that we could attach an electronic chip to his collection of books so he could track whose hands they transferred through and how many times they were read. He looked at me thinking I was crazy, but he recognized my witty acknowledgment of his fear. While this suggestion might be silly, think of it in terms of the peace of mind he would have knowing his books were being read and not added to a paper recycle bin.

Whether we fear the final resting spot of an item might truly be the end of its life, or we feel we have not fully discovered its meaning, discarding it might create an anxiety that is difficult to explain. I'll be honest: I still have Rod's grad-school papers. Maybe because I don't know what else to do with them, maybe because if I put them in the recycle bin they will be gone forever, maybe because they don't take up much space, or maybe because they're a window to the days before I met him – days I didn't ask enough questions about because of his early death. I honestly don't know. Probably a little of all of those things. The real irony is, I have never even read them.

Once our heart and mind are in sync with the concept that letting go of something does not equate to letting go of our memories, the process of finding peace and sorting through personal possessions can begin. When visiting a fellow widow's home several years ago, she shared with me her husband's "man room," a large bedroom located above their garage. The room showcased her husband's collection of toy cars, magazines, baseball hats, sports memorabilia, games, model airplanes, favorite books, trinkets from traveling, and so much more. This by far was the largest personal collection I had ever seen. In all my support of fellow widows, I had never experienced such a unique and meaningful array of physical items. Even without his physical presence, his possessions told a clear, vivid, and personal story. They were neatly organized, documented, and perfectly displayed, showcasing the deep-rooted relationship he had developed with each and every item. It was clearly his pride and joy, and I can only imagine how many happy hours he spent collecting, organizing, rereading, and tinkering around with this impressive display of passion. It was purely and simply a snapshot of him. Upon reaching her fifth-anniversary milestone of his passing, this woman felt the strength to start thinning and giving away his clothing stored in their bedroom closet. When I inquired about the trigger that allowed her to start the process, she shared a motto she established for herself: "If it will do good for someone else" then it was time to let go and allow someone else to benefit from it. It was truly a win-win for both her and the items' recipients. She had not yet tackled the man room, but she continued to ask the same question as she sorted through his other belongings. Not everything had to be sorted through at once, and I'm sure it will take her awhile to finally go through this monument to her husband. Nevertheless, she was starting her peace process.

There is a wide spectrum of beliefs about the healthiest ways to find peace and the associated importance of reconciliation of possessions. Our well-being and mental health are crucial, yet they are often compromised by the emotional toll we can experience when forced to make decisions involving our loved one's possessions. Some people need to hold on to items to feel connected, while others need to purge any semblance of their permanently altered future. I recently spent time with a woman who lost her husband to a complicated form of cancer. During our visit, she shared with me how wonderful their marriage was, how they were teammates in all areas of their lives – whether parenting their children, sharing similar hobbies, growing a vegetable garden, or reading the same book. They embraced life to the fullest, supporting each other's careers while moving from state to state when a new opportunity arose. Just when they were ready to settle into a more permanent arrangement, my client's husband was offered a unique opportunity in a different state.

As a couple, they chose to welcome the move as their first big adventure as empty nesters. With great excitement they moved, purchased a house, and carefully procured furniture they would be able to reuse in their retirement home. The first year of their journey was wonderful, spending time as a couple, exploring new areas, and traveling the world – until the life-changing day when he received a devastating diagnosis and soon succumbed to his aggressive form of cancer.

My client's life changed very suddenly; her future was unclear and her heart was broken. Unlike other widows I had worked with, she felt compelled to distance herself from their shared possessions. The thought of living their dream without him was too overwhelming. She preferred to sell or give away the items rather than save and embrace them. In her heart she wondered how she could sleep in their bed without him, how she could sit on their couch without him next to her, and how she could eat off their dishes if he was not there to share a meal with her.

As I listened, I had to admit she had a valid point of view. While her viewpoint is not my personal approach, and I could not relate to some of the decisions she made, this was her way of taking care of herself and her well-being. Her logic made sense. While she was in a tremendous amount of pain and making decisions on her own, she was aware of her actions and able to articulate what the next steps were for her. Finding peace was separating herself from their lost future together. At least for now.

FINDING PEACE WITH POSSESSIONS AFTER A LOSS

In life, we refer to our loved one's possessions as their "stuff" and "things." But in death, these "things" now signify forever-connections and cherished memories. Possessions represent self, love, passion, growth, maturity, happiness, sadness, endearment, and a priceless remembrance of a person's life and their time in this beautiful world. Just by holding them, their belongings provide us with warmth, togetherness, security, and an abundance of love. It is truly amazing to think how a toothbrush can hold so much meaning – an intimate part of someone's life, yet so simple.

The road to recovery has so many bumps and potholes that each jolt amplifies the reality of your current situation. Each crucial step in the process we've discussed so far – acknowledgment of the situation, facing fears, and understanding the importance of timing – are all are incredibly difficult to grasp. The collection of baseball hats that were once strewn across the closet, and to your dismay never quite made it back to their rightful place, have become sacred and no longer seem to be in the way. The cluttered office has become a sanctuary to just feel the presence of your loved one, and the backpack on the stairs is a visual gift after a long day. These are all welcome signs of their presence in your life and each item has become a special souvenir.

In my professional and personal life, I have been exposed to an array of different approaches of what do to, how to feel, and when to engage in the process. When Rod passed, our daughter was two years old and would jump on the couch every evening shouting, "Daddy out running, Daddy home soon!" Yet his running shoes were sitting by the door. It is hard to explain to a little one that if he were in fact running, he would have his shoes on his feet. One evening, as she repeated her evening ritual, something clicked emotionally with me, his shoes sitting by the door gave me a visceral feeling that he was right there with me. In that moment, I just knew his shoes would be staying by the front door for as long as I needed them to be there because they filled a small corner of the immense void I was currently in, and they could now become a symbol of him in our daily life. I would leave for work each day and say good-bye to Rod, and upon our return say hello as we entered the house. His shoes remained in the same place for a long time. Friends and family who came by would suggest I find a new home for them, expressing their discomfort in walking by shoes from a man eighteen months deceased. But that was their discomfort, not mine. Let's put it this way, they were uncomfortable, but I was shattered. My friends and family were welcome to share their opinion of my behavior choices; however, I was not moving the shoes until I felt comfortable moving them. In hindsight, I know they were questioning my ability to "get over" my loss as long as the shoes were by the door. Simple answer: there is nothing to get over, and we loved saying hello to Rod when we walked in the house after a long day. Those shoes allowed me to feel safe in my own home, and that's all that mattered.

When teaching a session of Facing the Mourning, a four-week grief support class, two attendees were a mother and daughter who had recently lost their son/brother prematurely in a skateboarding accident. Upon their arrival, I felt the weight of their pain and the distance between them. The first night's curriculum incorporated ideas for creating a loving memorial with your loved one's personal possessions. Neither mother nor daughter shared much that evening other than they were both devastated by the loss, and that their grieving styles were different. One of their points of contention was the bedroom. The mother kept her son's bedroom door closed because the pain was too great for her to see or touch any of his belongings. Meanwhile, the daughter wanted to sleep in his room, embrace his pillow, and look at all his things. The mother talked of plans to repurpose his room to an office, workout room, or craft room, while the daughter wanted desperately to leave it just as it was. We discussed ideas of how they could compromise, but when they left I could still feel the anxiety and tension between them.

But the next week, the pair walked into the group arm-in-arm, smiling and eager to share with the group what had transpired over the past week. They decided it was time to find peace, so they sat down and expressed their concerns with each other and, most importantly, listened with an open heart and open mind. The mother did not feel she could heal while the bedroom shouted to her that her son was never going to walk through its door again. The daughter shared that she needed his *belongings*, not necessarily his room, to help her cope with her loss. Taking our discussion from the previous week, they set out to determine how they could both satisfy their personal needs while supporting each other. Their openness in expressing their feelings and taking lessons from the session generated many ideas for next steps. The sister decided to create bookshelves in her bedroom using his collection of skateboards as shelves. Both chose T-shirts from his closet to make a quilt so each of them could cuddle with him, and they continued to box up remaining items that they believed would be comforting in the future. I fought back tears knowing that they found had peace with each other and his belongings.

The most frequently asked question I receive from friends, clients, and colleagues is about the appropriate time to take on the tasks associated with the belongings. The answer is simple: *when you are ready*. Undoubtedly friends and family members will push the griever to "think about" sorting through the items sooner than the griever wants to. And it makes sense. It is human nature to want to run from, hide, or remove those things that cause us the most pain. We often suppress and mask insecurities with drugs, alcohol, or other forms of distraction. How often do we choose to procrastinate or unintentionally leave the hardest task on our to-do list for last? And how often are we disappointed with ourselves for letting something hang over our head for too long? Our friends and family are just trying to help, but they aren't always going to get it right. From the outside, it would make logical sense that removing belongings from sight would alleviate a visual stressor and help a griever move forward.

After all, the phrase "out of sight, out of mind" is not without some supporting evidence from human psychology. But for many grievers, the haste to remove or clean through belongings will only solidify their new reality too quickly. Of course, there are exceptions to this; for example, when a move is imminent or an estate needs to be settled. Regardless, there is no malice on friends' and loved ones' part; they only want to help in the best way they can, based on their own experiences with coping.

Finding peace really takes shape when we begin to look at the next chapter of our lives. I am often asked when and how I started the process and how I found peace. For me, there was really no set time or specific trigger that started the process. It began slowly, with me wanting more space in the closet. So little by little I began bagging and boxing Rod's work clothes. This was an easier place to begin, as those articles of clothing did not carry sentimental value for me, and I thought others could use his suits, shirts, and work shoes. And I found a great organization whose mission was to help men get back on their feet by supporting their professional appearance. By no means was this the end-all with Rod's belongings; it was only the start, and a fairly innocent start that was relatively easy for me emotionally. And I knew that Rod would feel proud to help other men.

I began to wake up each day and think to myself that today was a good day to take some weight off of my shoulders and start the project so I could begin the next chapter of my life. Some days were more productive than others, but each day I gained confidence in the process and myself. Finding peace while sorting, thinning, and sharing personal possessions is a lifetime endeavor, a work in progress that will always be present. Items will be saved and repurposed, and some may go back in a box until the next time you are ready to confront them. The process is not straightforward. Individual experiences will differ. And most importantly, what you decide to keep or give away is your choice, and that may change in time.

I love sharing the poignant story of my daughter's crib because it provides insight into my emotional process, revealing the importance of finding peace with each item before you can find its new home. As I have shared, my daughter was only two years old when Rod died. When he was in town, their nightly ritual was for him to read her a story and place her in her crib for the night. The night before his death, he did just that. And that was the last night she ever slept in her crib. From that day forward I was unable to muster the strength to infringe on one of the final connections between father and daughter. Their last night together was theirs to cherish, and I wanted that moment to be captured forever. I knew she didn't remember, but I did, and I couldn't bear to tarnish that memory. Instead, we moved together into the guest bedroom until I was able to find a "big girl" bed. In my mind, I switched her from the crib to her new bed as a rite of passage, as she was "all grown up." I then covered the crib with blankets and moved it to the basement. The irony is that I saved the crib and continued to move it with the rest of our furniture for thirteen years. It was clear after a certain point that I would never actually *need* that crib again.

I never had more children, and none of my sisters ever asked to use it. But that didn't matter. The symbolism of a past family – my perfect threesome of a past family – was too strong to let it go. My husband, Taner, never pushed for me to sell or donate the crib. He never questioned my rationality as time passed, nor did he try to rationalize that our daughter doesn't remember those days. With each move he gently asked if the crib would be moving with us, even though he knew the answer would be yes.

In 2001, I embarked on an endeavor in metropolitan Denver to support those suffering a loss. I joined the board of directors of HeartLight Center, a grief and loss organization, as a founding member, later serving as executive director. While working closely with the president, Jennifer, we developed an incredible bond in our approach and commitment to serving our community. We had experienced significant life-changing losses at a similar time – for me, the loss of Rod, and for Jennifer, her father. We both had had corporate jobs in the past, and now we had a wonderful opportunity to use our experiences to help others honor very important people in their lives. One morning Jennifer shared with me that her daughter was expecting a baby, and they would be crib shopping later in the week. Before she could even tell me her schedule, I jumped out of my chair. It suddenly felt like a perfect time to find peace with the one thing I had yet to work through. I wanted to share the crib I had been moving for thirteen years with my connection to HeartLight Center. I had learned so much since Rod's passing, and I was finally using my knowledge to help others who were lost. I saw clearly that the time had come to close the circle and share the crib. Based on our mutual losses, the relationship Jennifer and I had created over the years was endearing, real, and extremely special because we were working together to help others deal with their own metaphorical cribs. I found peace moving the crib to its new home and thanked Rod and Jennifer's father for the gift of friendship, as our paths might not have otherwise crossed.

The crib is only one story of many rewarding, empowering, and fulfilling experiences I encountered when touching, feeling, and sharing my loved one's possessions. As I made calculated decisions about what to keep and what to give away, I felt a link to Rod that was endearing, as if he were with me helping me make the decisions about what to save for our daughter. I felt no judgment as I asked him what he would do if he were in my shoes and actually found humor in making up answers for him to help with my sense of accomplishment. Sure, I had fears of regretting my decisions, but I knew I was not alone making them, as he was next to me telling me I would be okay. He was my peace.

CHAPTER 3

ONE PIECE AT A TIME

It's time! Something has occurred that lets you know you are ready to begin the process of sorting, decluttering, thinning, sharing, or finding what you have been looking for – or maybe you're just sick of people pushing you to clean out your or a loved one's possessions. Whatever it might be, that trigger is going to help you move forward in finding peace, one piece at a time. The process of finding peace is a project within itself, and it will always be a work in progress, so you might not feel completely at ease as you embark on this journey. But with a little encouragement from your trigger, you will continue to build confidence and discover more peace along the way. You are ready to embrace the next steps of sorting the items, one piece at a time. You will quickly learn that the process is incredibly powerful, filled with strong emotions, strategies, mind games, pep talks, and a lot of patience.

The concept of one piece at a time is designed to encourage you to look at each piece and decide what to do with that individual item. It is also meant to eliminate the overwhelming sense of needing to complete a project in one sitting. After all, possessions weren't acquired in one day, so they definitely don't need to be sorted that quickly either. While there might be opportunities to clump things together as you sort, I advise instead that you to look at each item individually. And you never know what you might discover along the way if you take the time to slow down and try to enjoy the process. For example, if you were to think of a jewelry box of miscellaneous earrings, necklaces, and bracelets as one item, you would miss the opportunity to reconnect to the individual pieces; each piece of jewelry will have a different story.

For years, we used this process with Taner's parents who lived in the same large, four-bedroom house for more than forty years. As you can imagine, with that much square footage there is a lot of space to store clothing in closets, magazines in the basement, linens in drawers, flower vases in cabinets, boxes in the garage, and tools on the workbench. Most of the items in the basement no longer worked or had any relevant meaning, yet were relegated there because my in-laws were unable to part with them. My in-laws are part of a generation for whom saving items for future use was standard practice. An almost proverbial motto of that generation is, "You never know when you may need that [fill in the blank]." This can be hard for younger generations to understand when we are well versed in technology and one click away from access to almost anything we need.

Each time we visited, we would start the process of trying to find peace and parting with a few items. We would begin by sorting through their drawers and closets with the goal of taking a few carloads of their personal items to be donated to an organization in need. In the beginning, the process was smooth, as the things we donated didn't have a lot of emotional value. With both Taner and me available to do the heavy lifting, we emptied closets of old clothing, disposed of years of magazines, and cleaned out an array of household items: old vacuums, broken chairs, duplicate kitchen essentials, and so on. The process we developed of filling a few carloads on each visit worked well for years, with few hiccups. However, we started to encounter some snags when we began sorting the main floor. The mood would change, as the items here had more immediate meaning and were more visible on a daily basis. It was much easier to sort through those closets that were so far out of sight and mind. Here, my in-laws were resistant to giving away clothing that had not been worn in the past ten years, the briefcase that was used before retirement nearly twenty years prior, or miscellaneous paper in their home office that represented fifty years of correspondence, tax returns, financial and legal documents, photographs, saved articles, and more. These items were still germane in their eyes, and who were we to decide their fate during a quick visit? As we continued to try and help, we realized we needed to change our approach because they felt their life was fleeing out the door each time we visited.

We became increasingly careful not to be overzealous in one day. Instead, we spent more time engaging with them, asking questions about the origin of different objects and what their importance was. Most importantly, we tried to be as patient as possible, taking the time to allow them to share stories about photographs, books, scarves, jewelry, serving dishes, and other family heirlooms. We made sure the energy was upbeat, and when it wasn't we backed off. Through these visits, we learned that not all of their belongings held sentimental meaning, and those we were able to donate. We also learned that time of the day was important in maintaining their patience. We were wary of hunger and conscious of their daily routine so as not to interfere with their own priorities and sense of order. Although these cleansing sessions were exhausting – sometimes both physically and emotionally – the true gift for Taner and me was that we were able to sort and thin with them before it was too late. We heard stories we had never heard before and looked at items we had seen displayed for years with newfound appreciation. And we both have a greater appreciation and sense of guardianship for the items we have since inherited. Like many things in life, this was a process that took a long time, but with patience, we slowly made progress. Over the years my in-laws began grasping the idea that their greatest possessions were those they would want to share with their children and grand-children, rather than the one pair of shoes they wore to a holiday gathering. Understanding the triggers and points of contention allowed us to overcome mental roadblocks, work together as a family, and find new ways to encourage and celebrate accomplishments along the way. Remember, as with my in-laws, there is no shame in taking a much-needed break, adjusting your approach, and then marching ahead.

WHAT TO EXPECT

In order to truly anticipate and prepare for what is in front of you, you will need to set reasonable expectations, which should also include room for some emotional flexibility. The first step is to change your outlook by adopting a "Let's try this" rather than an "I can't" attitude. Rephrasing your beliefs can give you the bit of confidence you need to get started and allow you to celebrate a few accomplishments along the way. Instead of saying "I don't know how to do this," try "I will figure this out." Or "I don't know if I have the strength to do this," can become "Let's start and revisit later if I need to." As with most things in life, the anticipation of starting the process is much more nerve-racking than actually getting started. For some reason, we anticipate the worst, only to find great joy when reaching into the back of the closet or drawers and reliving memorable moments.

Unlike other household projects, this one can be easily derailed because the reason for the project is often far more emotionally charged than painting the walls, sprucing up a room, or hanging a television on the wall. Similar to a ball in a pinball machine, the feelings of being flipped up and down and all around are very common and very real. Nevertheless, know that you have the strength and tenacity to get it done. You have to believe in yourself and have confidence in your decision-making ability. If you experience a temporary setback, take the time you need by enjoying a break, taking deep breaths, finding a quiet place to meditate, going for a walk in the fresh air, having dinner with a friend, watching mindless television, or taking a warm bubble bath. But most importantly, clear the noise in your head and find your way back into the zone.

As we discussed, simply getting started can be the biggest hurdle, but once you get going, creating a reasonable plan will reduce frustration and anxiety (for more of the nuts and bolts of creating a plan, see the following section). As we know, Rome was not built in a day, nor will the belongings be sorted in a day – or a week, or even a month. What you are about to embrace is more than a project; think of it as a historical walk down memory lane. Take enough time to cherish the memories and feel the connection to both the person and their belongings. Finding a cadence that feels comfortable and productive is key in kicking off the endeavor. Any tactic that works is one you should embrace, whether it is moving from left to right around the room, playing a game with yourself in which you have to move five items before you take a break, or emptying one drawer. Sorting through personal belongings can also be comparable to tackling a box of puzzle pieces: each item needs to be sorted and handled before it ultimately finds its appropriate location. Regardless of the degree of difficulty or the number of pieces, each piece will find its home and so will your personal possessions.

Similar to working on a puzzle, some days are productive, while other days might feel more frustrating. And continuing the metaphor, like the edge pieces, the first day or first pass might have felt deceptively easy, but your momentum will undoubtedly ebb and flow. Try moving around the house as you would move around the puzzle table, which can provide a different viewpoint. On completion of the puzzle, you look at the finished product with pride, gratification, and fulfillment. The same feeling occurs as you make progress sorting through the possessions.

If you're apprehensive about starting, think of the process as a game and that you're looking for treasures. How many times have you cleaned out your junk drawer or vacuumed under your couch hoping to find treasures – those things you think you might have lost or haven't seen in years. Recently, while supporting a widower who was organizing his wife's belonging, I felt his uneasiness about starting as the process signified in his eyes that his wife was really gone. Still, he knew he wanted to start and needed my help. He mentioned his wife always hid cash in her shoes, purses, and socks, so I suggested that he look at the task as a game in search of treasures. The quest was to discover how many places his beloved had found to hide something small. This simple mind shift created the lighthearted purpose of searching for cash or any other prizes he could find. As we spent the afternoon together, he shared stories of his wife, allowing me to get to know her. Then, at the end of the day, we admired the pile of treasures we had found. In addition to some loose cash, we discovered at least thirty tubes of lipstick, enough pens to fill a shoebox, love letters, old birthday cards, misplaced jewelry, and enough gift cards for him to have dinner for two weeks. Our game provided a form of entertainment, which helped him manage his apprehensiveness and start on his own terms.

In my family, we created our own special tradition following my mother's untimely death. My father was eager to share Mom's belongings with his five daughters because he felt having a remembrance of her would help with the healing process. Our mom was not an accumulator of things, but there was certainly enough to split among us girls. He gathered pieces of her jewelry, clothing, and a collection of other personal belongings. While we were excited to receive a remembrance of our mother, we were skeptical of the impending process. Remarkably, all five of us had drama-free relationships, and we were rarely competitive with each other, yet we feared the process might not work. How would we divide the belongings fairly among five of us? Who would get to choose first? What if two of us wanted the same item? But our fears were tempered by an amazing process. During our next family gathering, our father placed Mom's items in the middle of the dining room table. When the five of us had gathered around, he suggested we proceed by taking turns selecting an item of interest to us. We placed our names in a hat to determine who would go first, and that sister would be followed by the sister to her right. We used this technique until all the items were selected.

The experience exceeded expectations as we shared amazing stories of our mother, some of which had never been told before. We started the process with fear and wound up with an experience that was soothing and created a new sense of sisterly bonding. When we got to an item that more than one of us was interested in, we decided that the person whose turn it was could keep it for a set period of time, and then later trade it so that we could all enjoy a beloved heirloom if we wanted. The process worked out perfectly and has led to a wonderful tradition for us that is still alive today. Every year each of us brings personal items we are no longer wearing, such as jewelry, scarves, or other articles of clothing, to a family gathering, and we swap. Just like with my mother's possessions, we place them on the middle of the table and take turns choosing something until all the items are gone. Not only are we giving new life to an old pair of earrings, we are sharing connections to our personal belongings. Some items resurface in future years, and some find their way to a donation bag; either way, we are honoring our mother, as the tradition started with her. The lessons from my mother's possessions taught my family that when you actively search for joy and tenderness with personal belongings, you are able to counterbalance the pain and anxiety of the loss.

When I created the list of who would receive selected items of Rod's belongings, I felt a sense of connection, warmth, and kindheartedness knowing that Rod's memory would exist with others through his possessions. His running buddy would run with his watch, his brother would participate in triathlons riding his bicycle, and his friends would wear his ties to work. In a new and lovely way, Rod was with us every day.

There is no doubt that decluttering, thinning, sorting, donating, and deciding what to do with your or a loved one's belongings is going to be hard. If it weren't, then we would all be living stress free in minimalist-style homes, and you wouldn't be reading this book. But objects and personal collections can have beautiful meaning, and the fact that you are struggling to cope with this monumental task means that you have lived and loved passionately. And that should not be taken lightly. Expect hardship and speed bumps. Expect to cry and be angry with yourself or a loved one. Expect to learn a little about a loved one or yourself. Expect to make great progress one day and none the next. But expect to be proud of both of those days. Prepare to celebrate your accomplishments, and be sure to create a set of goals to reward yourself along the way.

Building Your Game Plan: The Ten Essentials

You feel you are ready, you aim to be productive, you desire to be strong, you hope to avoid conflict with family members, and you crave a meaningful experience. All this can be achieved by building a game plan. A game plan will allow you to break down the unknown into smaller, easier-to-complete pieces, and you can now hold yourself more accountable. The Ten Essentials will provide direction, encouragement, and support.

Over the years, I have found that a trick I learned in high school from an amazing athletic coach helps immeasurably in creating a game plan. Their approach was to document your "hopes and fears." The idea is that by understanding your hopes and fears, you will be able to see where you have control. If you're aware of what you hope for, you can manage your expectations over the next couple of weeks, allowing space for your hopes to come true. The same can be applied to your fears. If you document your fears, you will do your best to conquer them. Before you begin, I encourage you to write down your hopes and fears and refer to them along the way. As you move along, feel free to reference your thoughts from day one and see how you are doing. Have any of your hopes and fears changed? What have you accomplished? Were the fears as prevalent as you thought they were going to be? To get you started, here are some common hopes and fears I have heard over the years:

- Hope that you feel the connection to your loved one

- Hope that the project will stay on course

- Hope that your team members (if you have them) will be helpful

- Hope that recipients will embrace the gifts you share

- Hope that the project will make you stronger

- Hope that the process won't be as overwhelming as expected

- Fear you may regret parting ways with an item

- Fear the project is too emotional

- Fear you will hurt someone's feelings by discarding a gift or heirloom

- Fear your item will be discarded by someone else

- Fear you won't have the patience to make decisions

- Fear you will give up and quit

- Fear your item will not find a good home

- Fear you and a family member may disagree

As with anything that requires courage, there will be times when you take three steps forward and then one backward. While this may be incredibly discouraging in the moment, simple math tells us that you are still two significant steps ahead of where you were yesterday. Similar to when players walk onto the playing field, the coach provides a game plan, words of encouragement, and the play list for the game. As your coach, I am providing you with a game plan with ten essential "plays." If you fall off the horse, get back on. If you are struggling to succeed, try again. And most importantly, believe in yourself.

1. ELIMINATE ALL EXCUSES

Say good-bye to your defenses, justifications, and rationalizations for not wanting to sort, thin, and redistribute your or a loved one's belongings. Find your peace and let go of your fear.

Frequently Used Excuses

Don't have time: The most common excuse is not having time. Like anything in life, we do have time if we make it. If time is stopping you from starting, you may want to engage your friends and family members who have asked on many occasions, "How can I help?" Secure their support in assisting with whatever you need to free up your time. How about caring for your children, carpooling to school or sports, mowing the lawn, cooking meals, or running errands? These opportunities will provide you with additional time and allow your friends and family to help you. It's time to realign your priorities or ask for help.

Don't know how: Another common excuse is not knowing how to tackle the project. Many people feel overwhelmed by figuring out where to begin, uncomfortable making decisions, indecisive about what to keep for the future, and may lack the confidence that they'll accomplish the task at hand. These insecurities often lead to resistance and procrastination. Folks may be entirely clear about what they want to accomplish, but they don't have the know-how to follow through. On many occasions, I have observed people struggle because they believed they didn't have the necessary skills to make good decisions. Yet I *know* we all have the ability to make those decisions, and often the most helpful thing is a bit of guidance from a special friend, a family member, a peer who is experiencing a similar situation, or a professional who can help guide you when you reach a stumbling block. There are so many people who want to help you be successful and are willing to throw you a life preserver. Catch it, and embrace the people around you who offer to help, as they will help lead you to make decisions and feel more confident in the process. They want to help keep you afloat.

Not necessary: Some people believe the process is just not necessary, making excuses not to embrace the task. Arguably this is true if the individual or family feel there fundamentally isn't a need. I have supported many people who have lost children and have not touched any of the belongings in their child's bedroom. To be honest, I am not sure if there is anything wrong with keeping the belongings. For them, perhaps it isn't an excuse but rather a yearning to be with their child through their belongings.

I have also spent time with individuals who don't believe it's necessary in the near term but will concede that someday it will happen. For instance, a colleague whose husband had passed away five years earlier recently attended my presentation on personal belongings. Her heart had been telling her there was no reason to sort through her husband's possessions as there was plenty of room in the closet for both of their clothing. She actually felt comfort having her husband's belongings next to hers. Up until this point, she didn't feel it was necessary to sort through the items; however, in the last year she had been dating someone special. She began thinking about letting someone else into her home and wanted to create a welcoming space for him. The attendees of the presentation provided encouragement for her to begin tackling the closet.

Fear of family dynamics: Family dynamics are especially complex when dealing with a death in the family. Yet it isn't one sibling being heartless or a spouse acting insensitively that causes the challenges; rather, family members are being provoked by heightened emotions and lack of practical reasoning. Further, most individuals tend to tiptoe around difficult circumstances rather than attacking them head-on. By asking a few probing questions, such as, "Mary, help me understand why,…" you can uncover what's driving the behavior rather than assuming you know. I especially like using that one line as an opener, as it allows the question's recipient to respond without being defensive. To ensure success, spend the necessary time with family members so you can answer each other's questions and concerns in advance.

I once received a call from a woman who had lost her mother. The provisions in her mother's will designated her as the executor of the estate, including the management of all her belongings. The woman needed help with deciding what to keep and what to save for other family members. As I was helping her determine how best to approach the project, she shared that she was very distraught over carrying out her mother's wishes. She had a sister with whom she had recently quarreled regarding her mother's end-of-life care, and now the two were estranged. Prior to the disagreement, they had had a wonderful relationship. Who, then, can blame the executor for making an excuse? Before she could fulfill her obligation to close the estate, my client first needed to resolve the fallout with her sister.

If there are any difficult family dynamics, I would encourage you to sit down with all parties and write down your hopes and fears as a group before addressing any specific possessions or plans for said possessions. In order the make the process efficient and meaningful for everyone, you all need to be on the same page and be honest with each other. As in the example above, it would be unfair for the executor to make decisions without considering the emotional journey of her sister, who is equally bereaved and equally in need of support and time to find peace.

2. WELCOME THE TRIGGERS

Triggers can sometimes cause an event or situation to happen, usually resulting in a change. In this case, you may be experiencing various triggers gently nudging you to consider rummaging through your or a loved one's personal belongings. My triggers for sorting through Rod's belongings were my daughter's questions about who the items belonged to and why we had them in the closets. Just as I knew something was changing in my life, you may be experiencing a similar feeling, yet for some reason you have hesitated to move forward. In my case, I wanted to stay with Rod in my refuge, our private space where we could be alone, just the two of us with all his comforting possessions. I ignored the triggers that were standing right in front of me so I could remain with him. I thought that if I walked into the closet or opened a drawer to share his belongings with others I would be saying good-bye forever. What I finally realized, however, was that I was in so much pain in the refuge that I needed to step out in the world to reconnect in a healthy way. And yet I still feel as if he is with me each and every day.

To help share my refuge, I explained the feeling on Day 88 of my book, *Living with Loss, One Day at a Time*. Without embracing the outside world, I would have not been able to take the next step.

Day 88
Grief Is a Refuge or a Battlefield

I found grief to be a refuge, a safe haven where I could be with my deceased husband. I was protected from the outside world as I hid in my personal shelter with him – our sanctuary to be alone together where only we could understand the pain.

The world outside my sanctuary was like a battlefield. A combat zone of my own thoughts and emotions where I hung at the front line, being attacked by my closest people hovering over me wanting me to get out of the war zone.

We all need a refuge from our grief, but we need the battlefield to win the clash.

To me, the triggers represent walking into the battlefield. If a trigger causes an event to occur – in this case beginning to look at the closets, drawers, piles, toys, and personal items differently – then maybe it is time to embrace the trigger.

Sometimes just one trigger is not enough, sometimes you might need two. Listen when you hear them, respond when you see them, and integrate them together to help you walk into the battlefield.

The Most Frequent Triggers

- One day you wake up with a feeling that "today is the day I am ready to start." Nothing atypical happened – maybe you had a dream, maybe you read something in a book the night before, or maybe it was just a feeling that you finally chose to appease.

- You start encroaching on your loved one's side of the closet as you need a bit more room to hang your clothes or put sweaters on shelves. To avoid feeling too cluttered you decide to start pulling out a few items that don't carry sentimental value or items you have never really been fond of. That's all you needed to start.

- You have been in search of something in the office such as an old tax return, medical document, travel documents, or a photograph, so you find yourself sorting and making piles. You have a pile of papers to be shredded, a pile to discuss with your kids, and a pile to refile. You have begun.

- You have a desire to get your house back. You lived with your father during his final days, and his medical equipment – including a bed, oxygen tank, and a variety of medicines – are in your kitchen, spare bedroom, and bathroom. You are yearning for your home to no longer look like a hospital, so the process begins.

- The seasons have changed, you are recovering from your loss, so you have chosen to spruce up your family room. You have a desire to reengage with friends and want to feel good about your home. As you start the process of sprucing, you move one item to a bedroom, grab something from a different bedroom to replace the item you just moved. Now you place something in a donation pile, then you're in the closet adding something else to a donation pile, and before you know it, you have reached a goal of 10,000 steps in your own home. Your first action led to the second, which led to the third, creating a rhythm.

- Winter is lurking around the corner, and you have a burning desire to park your car in the garage. But that's where you're storing your parents' belongings – the ones that didn't fit into their smaller apartment when they downsized. When they moved, you boxed up what you believed would be items to save and stored them in your garage. Now, as you begin to consolidate the boxes, you decide to donate a few more items, share special mementos with grandchildren, and swap out a few items at your parents' new home. You embraced the trigger and your car is now in the garage.

- You always wanted an in-home gym but didn't have the space for it. With the recent changes in your personal life, you're now ready to repurpose a room. In order to overhaul that back bedroom, you have to start by clearing out the closets, designing the layout, and selling the furniture currently in the room. The desire to take care of yourself triggered the process.

- The most common trigger among our aging population is the feeling of clutter. Your saving has crept into the extra closets, the dining room table is covered with junk mail, your shelves in the garage have tools you no longer need, and your kitchen has cookware that you haven't touched in years. Your trigger in this case is that you want to welcome family to visit and celebrate the next holiday, which means you need to clear off the table and declutter the kitchen to prepare a wonderful feast.

- Your grandchild is leaving for college, and you would like to share one of your spouse's belongings with her before she leaves. As you dig through their possessions, you feel your gift to her would exclude your other grandchildren, so you decide to find something for each grandchild.

- Another common trigger is a winter coat drive. Most cities have a coat drive in the fall, regardless of the climate. In my area, a local dry cleaner chain places a large box in their entryway where you can drop off coats for others who are less fortunate. There is something comforting knowing you have helped someone else by providing a warm coat. Next you decide to share gloves, a hat, and shoes.

- For many, the dining room table takes over as the staging area for papers, items you don't know what to do with, or keepsakes requiring a storage solution. In your quest to find your dining room table in preparation for hosting a dinner, you have two choices: sort the items or box them and move them to another room. The trigger of hosting a dinner helps you choose to sort the items.

- A local charity is sponsoring a fund-raiser and is in need of auction items. Your basement is filled with professional sports memorabilia. While you have enjoyed the themed walls for years, the excitement of sharing these things with someone else could be your trigger to free up wall space for something else. Ease into the process by choosing items of less interest to you, then donating them and taking a tax deduction.

- The paper piles are taking over your house. At one time, you knew how to manage new mail, catalogs, bank and utility statements, coupons, and bills within your controlled chaos; however, you no longer know which pile is which. Your methodical way of adding to the piles has failed you. Therefore, it's time to sort through the piles and dispose of or shred what you no longer need.

- The most overwhelming yet effective trigger is the need to move to a new home with a fixed deadline. Acknowledge the trigger, and do the best you can sorting and clearing items that have no sentimental or monetary value. Box what you have to and revisit when the time is right. In this case, breathe, relax, and take care of you.

- The day has arrived when your parents have asked you to help them move to a smaller place. That is both a blessing and a curse. They need your help and you are ready to provide it. Use the helpful hints in this book, and try to make meaningful decisions in an empathetic way. Be assertive while being understanding. Most importantly, work on your negotiating skills in order to be successful.

Now that you've embraced the triggers, it's time to be wary of the common pitfalls you many encounter along the way.

3. AVOID PITFALLS

There will always be obstacles and unforeseen consequences when making decisions about what to do with possessions. What you do when you encounter them is the key to dealing with your anxiety. Addressing pitfalls proactively is crucial to your success. Instead of allowing the traps or hazards to derail you, watch for them. When you encounter one, jump over it or drive around and continue down the road.

Succumbing to Outside Influences Before You Are Ready

People who have not experienced a loss or have not supported aging parents are unaware of the emotional impact related to sorting through personal belongings. It is difficult to truly understand the pressures and emotional toll these journeys can take. Keep in mind that some of these people may try to sympathize and help, but their preconceived ideas about how to go about it just don't apply to your situation as easily as they might think. Ultimately, of course, they mean well and are simply trying to encourage you to find peace.

Your individual journey is unique to you. If two adults experience a similar loss, their first instinct is to compare journeys; however, the circumstances of the loss, the access to family support, and what occurs behind their front door likely differ and result in related but distinct experiences. With that said, would it be fair to say they should both start at the same time?

Make sure you're not starting before you're ready just because others are pressuring you to. Allowing others to influence you to the point where you're questioning yourself can result in the following pitfall: starting too soon.

Giving Away an Item Too Fast

One significant pitfall my clients have experienced is giving away items too fast. I longed for many of Rod's items once I had given them away – mostly the items that would have provided our daughter more insight into her father.

The reckoning came when my daughter saw a picture of her father playing a guitar. At the time, she was taking flute and piano lessons and was now yearning to learn yet another musical instrument. She asked me where the guitar was, and I shared that the old, unstrung, and out-of-date guitar was at her uncle's house. She wanted it, even though I continued to explain its poor condition and that she could rent a newer, more reliable guitar if she really wanted to learn how to play. But my rationale didn't appease her; she specifically wanted Rod's guitar. In that moment, I realized I had given away the guitar too soon without thinking that one day my daughter might want it. Fortunately, I felt comfortable reaching out to my brother-in-law to rectify the situation, and he immediately retrieved the guitar from the attic. Although she was disappointed when she saw the condition it was in, she nevertheless had to see it herself and formulate her own opinion.

While I thought I had made the right decision in providing each of Rod's siblings with a memorable gift, I now question if I should have saved more for my daughter. It's complicated when identifying items for specific recipients, the most difficult being younger children who have lost a parent. How do you know what they will want? How do you know the item will have meaning? When in doubt, be sure to save them. I was fortunate that the guitar was still close by, but not everyone always is.

Allowing Your Deceased Loved One to Make the Decision for You

One area of vulnerability is making decisions based on what you think your loved one would want you to do. This approach is usually based on speculation, even if you had the opportunity to discuss these potential circumstances before they passed.

The evening that Rod passed away sitting in his car in the office parking structure changed my relationship with our car. I never wanted to see it again, yet I knew he would have wanted me to keep the newer, more reliable car. I just couldn't do it. I asked a tow company to bring the car to a relative's house where it sat for a while waiting for me to "come to my senses." I listened to Rod in my head, coaching me on what is best for me. But the reality was, how would he know? His ideals were based on practicality, money, and safety. Had I followed his "advice," I would have suffered from the sadness the car conjured. Instead, I followed my heart and sold the car.

This can be a slippery slope, as you want to honor your loved one in decisions moving forward, yet the circumstances are different now. Take the time to think through your decisions, especially the ones that carry more emotional value. Rod didn't have any sentimental connection to that car specifically, so I was able to override his voice in my head without regret.

4. PRIORITIZE WHERE TO BEGIN

Whether you are attempting the project yourself or accompanied by family members, prioritizing where to begin is important. Although there are different schools of thought, I will share the one that I have found to be most successful. As you read the following, visualize your own space.

My suggestion is to start in a place where you can comfortably move the items around with a bit of ease without creating piles in a walkway – perhaps the garage or the corner of a basement. Both of these areas are most likely home to the items that are easy to deal with. It's likely they have been tucked away for a while, so they might be quicker to sort through. Also, if you are out of the main area of your living space, you can take a break without seeing the piles, having to climb over them, or being constantly reminded of the project. A woman attending one of my group sessions shared that her starting point was the drawers in her husband's office. She placed his papers in boxes, and before she knew it she was literally trapped in the office by boxes. While it may sound silly, you can get in a groove before you look up and realize how illogical your approach may have been.

Once you have decided where to begin, create a list of all the places in your house where you would like to sort, rebox, or prepare piles for donations. Be sure to include all the bedrooms, outdoor space, office, garage, storage units, attic, a friend's home, shed, or any other place where personal belongings have been stored. Then take a break, and when you come back, prioritize the list based on emotional impact, potential triggers, and the physical support you may need from your friends or family.

5. CHOOSE A START DATE

Only you can decide when the appropriate time is to start the project. Each person's unique circumstances will dictate when they need to begin. Unless you are forced to begin by an external trigger such as a pending move, there is no set time, but once you do feel ready, set a date and put it in your calendar. This will eliminate any further excuse to procrastinate. Whether it is just for you or you are planning with others, make this date something to celebrate. Start with a favorite dinner the night before or a full breakfast in the morning. Make a good playlist and pick out a few of your favorite snacks to enjoy along the way as rewards for your progress.

When tasked with sorting through your loved one's personal possessions following a loss, the start date will vary in part based on the circumstances surrounding the loss. When experiencing a sudden death, the family is ill-prepared and their priorities are consumed with coordinating logistics and managing paperwork. In the case of a long-term illness, however, the family may have started the process of thinning and distributing belongings while caring for their loved one.

In following the steps of the Ten Essentials, it is important not to start too quickly in order to avoid some of the pitfalls discussed. If possible, my recommendation is to wait at least three to six months, which will allow you the time needed to understand the impact of the loss and begin the healing process.

In preparing to downsize a home or relocate aging parents, the process can start at any time. In fact, the earlier the better. Not waiting allows for a less rigorous move down the road, especially when assisting aging parents. Keep in mind that aging parents may blame their children for the pending move, accusing them of being overbearing or aggressive. In most cases, however, the reaction has less to do with the children and more to do with the difficulty of leaving familiar surroundings or accepting their new reality.

6. BUILD YOUR TEAM

The thought of attempting the project alone is daunting. If you're so inclined, having the right people around you to help provide support and encouragement can result in greater success. This is your tribe, the people who know you and have the ability to encourage you. And those individuals are the ones you should trust while you are vulnerable. The suitable team member will follow your lead and guide you to make informed decisions. They are your trusted confidants that balance your need for camaraderie, support, and a lot of patience.

As in sync as you might be with your team, an important factor to remember is that they cannot read your mind, especially on such a momentous occasion. This means that communicating your needs ahead of time is essential. If you are more productive earlier in the day, be sure to request that the team work in the morning. If you are a three-meal-a-day plus snacks person, be sure to have a team member arrange for food. If music is a motivator, find the right genre to motivate and soothe the team. If you are reenergized by fresh air and sunshine, be sure to have your team send you outside.

Should you decide to build a team, evaluate all the people who have offered their assistance and determine how helpful they will be. As you create your list, be sure to include their skill sets. While you want a few take-charge people, bear in mind that too many may create unwanted drama or tension.

Potential Team Members

A trustworthy confidant: The special team member who will guide you when making sentimental decisions. They will find the balance of helping you while comforting you. Their intuitive nature helps anticipate your needs before you know you need something, allowing you to focus on the job at hand.

The workhorse: This strong, physical, hardworking person could be referred to as the "runner." This person is willing to carry boxes to the car, garage, or basement. In addition, they are great at accepting direction without interfering with the decision-making or questioning judgment.

The organizer: This is the spreadsheet coordinator, the person who excels at making phone calls, arranging pickups, and photographing and documenting items. Known as the "checker off-er," this person ensures nothing falls through the cracks. No detail is too small or too large.

The packer: This person is great at – you guessed it – packing. They have incredible space awareness, can fit an astonishing amount into small spaces, and know how to protect valuables. They can be instrumental in helping the workhorse maximize time or help keep things organized as you create your six piles, which are discussed in the next section.

The coordinator: The "parent" team member who takes care of the team providing nourishment, managing the schedule, and adding humor when necessary. They act as the team leader, communicating, assigning responsibilities, and advising friends and family members when they are needed.

Fulfilling the above roles can be accomplished with a handful of people. If you have a team, the number of members will depend on the flexibility in scheduling and whether you use of a coordinator to help direct the team. The most important person on the team is you; if you are tired, overworked, or hungry, the productivity will be compromised. And remember, embarking on the journey alone is doable; however, if you have any doubt, encourage yourself to reach out – even if it's just to one other person. You may find that having support really helps keep you steady, on task, and feeling supported.

When the time came for me to sort Rod's belongings, building a team was a foreign concept. I preferred working alone so I could be with Rod, just the two of us touching each piece together, one piece at a time. Besides, I couldn't imagine who would want to fill trash bags or haul his stuff to a donation center. I later learned that I had a team of people who would have jumped at the opportunity to participate had I asked. I found there were many tasks I could have delegated that would not have interfered with my private time with Rod.

In the end, no matter what the size of your team, remember that ultimately *you* are in charge, so don't be afraid to use your voice when you feel overwhelmed or need a break.

7. CREATE A TIMELINE

In essence, you are creating a project plan. The key elements to the plan are the start date, proposed finish date, number of people available to help, and the size of the project. Once these variables are defined, the plan can be created. Personally, I am a big supporter of spreadsheets because of their ability to sort, update, track, and add detail to the plan. If you decide to use a spreadsheet, I recommend creating the following columns:

- Date when the room will be addressed

- Name of each room (e.g., bedroom, kitchen, garage)

- Detail of item

- Save, share, donate

- Name of recipient

Once you have completed the timeline, add 20 percent more for unforeseen delays. I am a firm believer in project plans, as the visual timeline provides a blueprint of the project. It's also a great tool to communicate with others and capture changes as they occur.

8. IDENTIFY POTENTIAL RECIPIENTS

Make a list of people who have entered your or a loved one's life and have left a lasting impression and a lifetime connection. These are the people you or your loved one have shared a special experience with, people with whom you would like to share a personal belonging. Your list may include children, grandchildren, aunts, uncles, siblings, friends, neighbors, coworkers, schoolmates, members of your congregations, or future family members.

The list is a work in progress, as you may choose to add or subtract names over time. Once the list is created, I recommend arranging the names in order of significance, as this will allow you to focus on the most important people first. Now make another list, this one of items you have identified in advance. Both lists can be maintained in a spreadsheet or Word document with columns, allowing for easy updates and sorting. Of course, some people may prefer the use of a legal pad and a pen. Whatever your preferred method, on completion of your two lists place them side by side. This will allow you to match a person to an item.

The process of creating my two lists allowed me to identify items I was ready to share immediately. Rod was an avid runner and triathlete, and I had ideas of how to keep him racing with me. That said, the feeling of his bicycle hanging in the garage just didn't feel right, so, as I've mentioned, I shared his bicycle, nicknamed Stella, with his older brother so he would continue his legacy by racing in local events. Similarly, with his running watch, who better to be wear it than his running buddy? I loved the thought that they were still running together. And the most special gift was for Rod's dad, who arrived at our house unaware he would be attending his son's funeral. When he asked if he could borrow one of Rod's ties for the service, I searched for the most poignant tie to share. I chose the tie Rod was wearing when he passed away. To me, his father was the perfect match for such an important and meaningful piece of clothing, and he's has worn that tie to every wedding and funeral since. As I completed this process, I realized that sharing specific items immediately provides both people with the opportunity to begin the healing process.

For those who like to plan proactively, a current trend among family members is to identify recipients of possessions in advance. I have witnessed families spend time together sorting through family heirlooms, identifying who will get what when the parents pass. They document the process by creating a book with pictures and information relating to each item. There are great advantages to this approach, the greatest being that the family spends time together embracing the inheritances and learning firsthand about the history of each item.

9. CREATE AN "ELEVATOR PITCH"

An "elevator pitch" is quick way to tell your story. Creating a clear, brief, and well-thought-out pitch that communicates the status of your belongings is a proactive way of managing the people around you who are pushing a bit too hard. Although these people are well-meaning, you may not be ready to battle their advances. By being prepared with your elevator pitch in advance, you will remain poised and self-assured when asked questions.

In most cases, the people around you are asking questions and voicing their concerns because they care about you, not because they are criticizing your approach or progress. Yes, they have their opinions; however, their comments are based in encouragement, not criticism. Unfortunately, the receiver often responds defensively, interpreting such comments as a form of disapproval. When people ask how you are progressing, take the time to present your well-rehearsed elevator pitch. You will be amazed at the response.

In writing the ideal pitch, be concise so that you can present your perspective within thirty seconds. Be sure to include your sense of accomplishment and appreciation for those who are supporting you. Or better yet, just tell them you are following the advice, techniques, and practices of a book you are reading – *Finding Peace, One Piece at a Time.*

10. THE JOURNEY IS YOURS TO EMBRACE

You now have all the necessary tools to begin. Most importantly, as you embark on the Magic of Six Piles, explained in the following section, you have established a framework to be successful. Be humble, find joy, and embrace the journey you're about to begin. Trust your intuition, accept the help and support that others offer you, and try not to let insecurities get the best of you. Don't lose sight of your goals, because ultimately this process is going to improve your life in some capacity. And there is never harm in revisiting your hopes and fears list to reinspire you (see p. 55).

Magic of Six Piles

Your game plan is complete. You have prepared by using the Ten Essentials, and now the starting whistle is about to blow. As you go from room to room, section to section, and piece to piece, adhering to a methodology that I call the "six piles" can help you realistically achieve your personal goals. Using this approach, you will find the process to be fulfilling, comfortable, and straightforward.

How does the magic occur? By touching an item only once. Try to visualize yourself standing in a room or in front of an open drawer. As you look down on all the items, take the item closest to you, reminisce how and why this item has come into your life, place it in the correct pile, and grab the next item.

Each pile has a purpose and can be identified as:

Keep: The items you would like to keep for yourself or your children

Share: The items you want to share with a friend or family member

Donate: The items you would like to donate to an organization dedicated to furthering a particular social cause

Sell: The items that have monetary value

Dispose: The items that are considered trash or recyclable

Ponder: The items that you are not comfortable
   placing in the first five piles

The best way to begin is by clearing a section in the
room you chose to start in. Be sure the space is large enough
for six piles. Using paper, sticky notes, or labels, identify the
piles for yourself and, if applicable, your team members.

Now it's time to read the helpful hints, create the
piles, and get going!

HELPFUL HINTS

In this section, you'll discover wonderful tips and tricks
to help you sort through a closet or drawer. While these
ideas are simple, they are instrumental in assisting you to
reach your goals. And as you acquaint yourself with them,
you'll find that they create a unique jargon specifically for
sorting personal possessions – a special language to share
with your team if you wish.

Work right to left or left to right: In other
words, don't jump around. If you have chosen a
closet to begin the process, start on the far right
and proceed toward the left (or vice versa). This
technique is efficient for organizing and cleaning
projects, as it allows you to see the progress you're
making. Think of cleaning up after a holiday
meal: all the dishes are piled up around the sink.
You begin tackling the pile on the left side, move

clockwise to the right, and watch chunks of clutter disappear as you progress. You can create the same visual in a closet.

Don't leave the room empty-handed: One of my favorite sayings is, "Why should you backtrack unless you're purposely counting your daily steps to reach your exercise goal?" Here the idea is that while you're running around the house sorting items, grabbing something to eat, making a phone call, or just taking a much-needed break, be sure never to leave the room you are working in empty-handed. There is always something to throw in the trash or to recycle, a box to bring to the garage, or an item to be placed in the correct closet or drawer. Make the most of your forward steps.

Use the concept of thinning rather than cleaning: The thought of cleaning is often perceived as something you have to do with a sponge and can of cleanser rather than a project you are embarking on that may or may not have a clearly defined finish line. If you adopt the theory of thinning rather than cleaning, you will be much more engaged and successful. (Of course if you're so inclined, take the opportunity to clean as you go, too!) When tasked with "cleaning" a closet, you may think it has to be cleared of all belongings. This can lead to hesitation, or even halt the process, as you're just not ready to make final decisions.

But with thinning, it's acceptable to add items to a PONDER PILE (see p. 113), allowing for items to be left in the room. Note: there may be someone on your team – or even you yourself – who looks at the two concepts as an issue of semantics, and arguably this is correct; however, the concept of thinning is much less stressful than cleaning.

Tackle one room at a time: Choose the area of your house where it makes the most sense for you to begin. Do your best not to deviate from that room. Similar to housecleaning, our natural instinct is to immediately "fix" whatever we see that needs attention. For example, you've started thinning the spare room. You find something that needs to go to the laundry room, and while you're there, you see folded laundry ready for you to put away. So you take the laundry to a bedroom and open the dresser drawers. But then you decide to start thinning out *those* drawers before you actually put the clean clothes away. And… soon you'll be deep into other nearby projects, but you won't have accomplished thinning that first bedroom. Working in multiple rooms simultaneously might feel like you are making progress; however, this approach can make the rooms feel like a tornado struck, leaving chaos that can become difficult and confusing to work with.

Develop a cadence: Once you have a rhythm, try to stay with it for as long as you can. Avoid taking a break or getting preoccupied with someone or something else for as long as you can. Try to eliminate distractions. For example, keep in mind that, although it may be tempting to have the TV on for background noise and company, it is easy to get sidelined by what's on the screen. If you prefer to work in a less quiet environment, turn on your favorite music. We all know how energy can be sucked out of a room, interfering with your rhythm and forward progress, so focus as much attention as possible on the task at hand. Keeping a decent cadence is key to providing energy and momentum to reach your objectives for the day.

Touch an item only once: As you start right to left/left to right in your chosen space, be sure to touch each item only once. When you make contact with an item, determine which of the six piles the item in your hand should be placed in. If you're waffling, put it in the PONDER PILE (see p. 113). Avoid the temptation to put it back where it came from just to keep from having to make a decision.

Set a time limit for each item: This is truly a great way to keep on track. If you set a time limit for determining an item's pile, you'll stay on track. For example, set the per-item time limit to two minutes. That should permit enough time to reminisce and to conclude which pile it belongs in. There will, of course, be items that take less than thirty seconds, while others will stretch past the two-minute warning. You can borrow time from a previous item as long as you keep the same cadence.

No deviating until you place five items in the piles: This is a fun game you can play with yourself to maintain forward momentum. For example, before you can look at your cell phone you need to place five items in a pile; or each hour your goal is to place fifty items in the appropriate piles; or you can't have lunch until the bedroom is complete. Believe it or not, inventing games to get through the items is an awesome motivator.

Dispose of average possessions: If you find an item to be outdated, average at best, of no use, or you decide that it's simply something you have been carrying with you for too many years, it's time to add it to the SHARE or DONATE PILE (see pp. 98 and 102). When in doubt, ask yourself a few questions, including, "Does the item bring me happiness?" "Will the item help others?" "Is there a home that could better use this?" If it does not bring you joy, happiness, or make you feel great, get rid of it, especially since it just takes up space. Let someone else benefit from thinking the item is awesome.

Follow the process of the Magic of Six Piles: The true magic is when you follow the ideas defined in the Magic of Six Piles, described in the following section. Each of your items has an appropriate home in one of those six piles. Keep in mind that you can revisit the KEEP and PONDER PILES (see pp. 89 and 113), while the others may not be recoverable.

THE SIX PILES

PILE #1 – KEEP

The KEEP pile is the most sentimental of the piles, consisting of all the items you would like to hold on to for yourself or your children. These are special items that have been part of your or your loved one's life journey. They tell a specific story and preserve special memories for you.

When sorting through Rod's belongings, I was able to part ways with his clothes at a steady pace. His T-shirt collection provided an emotional journey down memory lane, so I struggled a bit over what to keep and what to share. I felt less of a connection to his suits, shoes, and other work clothes, which allowed me to box those items without hesitation. Once I found a rhythm, I was able to choose what I wanted for myself and what I thought my daughter would appreciate in the future. The remaining items of clothing were placed in the DONATE PILE. I will admit, my KEEP and PONDER PILES (see pp. 89 and 113) swelled as I added more items than I thought I wanted; however, this was my first pass, and I knew I could revisit both piles in the future. My suggestion, then, is when in doubt, keep it; be cautious about not giving items away too fast. You will find that it is much easier to take a second pass than try to track down a donated item.

As I created my KEEP PILE, I struggled most with what I called the "nonconventional" items. These were things that didn't belong in the trash but had no purpose for anyone else – in some cases, including me. They were seemingly random pieces of Rod that I wanted to save so I could hold on to him forever. My friends and family must have thought I was pretty peculiar when they saw some of the items in my KEEP PILE. It didn't matter, it wasn't about them, it was about me (and Rod). The pile of the nonconventional items became the genesis of Rod's box – my treasured memorial of Rod and his life. To this day, each time I open the box, I am able to see him, feel him, smell him, and just be with him. The box also serves as an introduction to the people who never met Rod, including my husband, Taner, who has learned so much about Rod from the box. At the time, even I thought it was a bit odd when I added a variety of what seemed to be arbitrary items to the box, but now I am so thankful that I listened to my heart, not logic. Each item is neatly placed in the box, and on top, there is a pair of salmon-colored children's shoes. I have been asked many times why I would save a pair of little girl's shoes in a memory box for Rod. For me the answer is simple, although the reason is complicated: my daughter was wearing those shoes the day Rod passed. I was holding her in my arms looking down when I heard the heart-wrenching news. I remember that all I saw was her shoes.

Below is a list of the items I put in Rod's box. To this day, they provide me with comfort and warmth as I recall both Rod and our life together.

Random Possessions in Rod's Box

- His passport, detailing all the wonderful places in the world we had traveled to together

- His business card, showcasing his last job – an indication of how successful his career would have been

- His driver's license, recognizing that it had expired and would never be renewed

- His running log, documenting his runs. This is one of my favorite items to revisit, as the log is physical rather than digital, allowing me to see his handwriting.

- His wallet, containing his expired airline, medical insurance, and credit cards

- His eyeglasses, reminding me of all the nights I moved his glasses on the nightstand so he would search for them in the morning. I still chuckle to this day that he never realized I moved them.

- The framed photos of our family that sat proudly on his desk

- The *Wall Street Journal* printed on the day he passed

- The Kansas City phone book, which was the last time his name ever appeared in one

- The shoes our daughter was wearing when we went to the hospital, the item I was staring at when I heard the devastating news that he had passed

- The pine cone from our hike on Twin Sisters Mountain with family and friends when we scattered his ashes

- The T-shirts from all his marathons

- The condolence cards we received, sharing thoughtful sentiments from friends and colleagues

Of course, the contents of Rod's box are what I chose as my keepsakes, a potpourri of items offering me a special sense of connection. If you were to create a box, your items would naturally differ, but you might experience a similar reaction when you opened the lid.

Over the years, I have witnessed an array of creative, loving, and meaningful remembrances created by family members from their loved one's possessions. I remember one in particular that was unique and extremely poignant: a wooden stationery box created by a widowed woman who attended one of my programs on creating a memorial tribute. As part of the assignment, the group was tasked with resolving a personal challenge they encountered when sorting through their loved one's belongings. The widow shared that she was challenged by the belongings in the couple's home office. She found it impossible to shred papers with her husband's signature because she found comfort in seeing his handwriting. She then came up with the idea to capture his signature as part of her memorial tribute. She purchased a wooden stationery box from a hobby store; gathered her husband's signature from old checks, financial documents, and signed cards; and affixed them in a collage on the box. She created a functional piece of emotional art, storing her husband's wedding ring, wallet, and other keepsakes inside and displaying it proudly on her dresser.

Your KEEP PILE contains items that will be incorporated into your closet, your drawers, or somehow repurposed in your home. Many find comfort in wearing old clothes, displaying certain objects on shelves, or using items in the kitchen – upcycling or repurposing them to add a new meaning. I have found that the most common traditions are wearing a loved one's piece of clothing or jewelry, writing with their favorite pen, using their sports equipment, or drinking from their coffee mug. As you sort, engage in a bit of creativity, as there are many ways to repurpose items to suit your or your family's individual tastes.

Here are a few ideas:

- Create a quilt using fabric pieces from your loved one's clothing. When designing the quilt, you have the option of telling a life story or creating a comfort blanket for you and other family members. It can be truly magical when the clothing touches your skin, giving you a feeling of warmth and contentment.

- Design a "wall of fame" honoring a family member by telling their story through photographs. You can begin by capturing their childhood, teenage, and young adult years. As the story progresses, add photographs of other life milestones, chronologically sharing their history. You can display the photographs on a wall using a collection of standard frames, creating a neat and tidy arrangement, or you can use an assortment of frames in a gallery-wall style. However you choose to display the photographs, the wall will honor a loved one.

- Repurpose a piece of jewelry by resetting a gemstone in an age-appropriate or fashionable design. If you have a vision of what you would like the new piece to look like, bring a drawing or a picture to a jeweler. They can help you reset, redesign, or incorporate several pieces together to create a perfect keepsake.

- Create a shadow box or cabinet displaying keepsakes from childhood, military memorabilia, or family heirlooms. There is no better way of memorializing someone than being able to showcase special remembrances and share them with others.

When younger children are impacted by a loss, they are not in a position to determine what is best to keep, relying instead on a parent or guardian to decide. While I struggled with what to save for my daughter, I knew my main goal was to provide her with a snapshot of her father through his belongings. I wanted her to experience his personality, his humor, his silliness, and his love for both of his special ladies. Since she was so young, I placed items for both of us in Rod's box to share forever. But one of my dear friends took a different approach. After her husband passed, she created individual boxes for each of her children. She personalized the items based on his relationship with each child, including photos, a special hat, and a pair of socks from his huge collection.

There is a significant difference between creating a KEEP PILE when downsizing a home and creating one after the death of a loved one. While the process might be similar, the decisions about what to keep differ, especially if there is more than one person involved in the process. In the case of aging parents, one person might want to move a household of books, while another may not want to use the limited space for bookshelves – she may prefer to fill the shelves with family photos and trinkets instead. What is valuable to one person may not have the same value to someone else. And when defining value, it's not only about monetary worth but also about significance, usefulness, meaning, and benefit. These differing views may complicate what will be added to the KEEP PILE. So who gets to decide what to keep, and how do you resolve the conflicting views? The china place settings are just one example. What about the sterling silver serving set that has been passed down for multiple generations? Perhaps start by each person choosing a set number of things to keep, and the other can't question the decision. You can continue to sort the rest of the items, or put them in the PONDER PILE for later once you see how the size of the KEEP PILE adds up.

Especially when a couple or multiple family members are involved in the downsizing decision-making process, there may be a difference of opinion about what should be moved to the new living arrangement versus what shouldn't. I experienced this firsthand on a recent visit to my eighty-five-year-old neighbor's home, where I found myself playing referee to two very different points of view about what would move to a new home and what should be donated or discarded. The couple has been married for fifty-five years, and while neither of them were terminally ill, the wife was preparing their home for a future move. As they moved from room to room, they had been very successful and were in agreement on what to do with most items. The one item that created a stumbling block was the husband's box of memorabilia, which included childhood keepsakes, college yearbooks, awards, and other treasures from his life's journey. She felt the box had no value, but he clearly disagreed and was struggling to articulate why he wanted to save these items.

As the three of us sat at their kitchen table discussing what to keep, I felt as if I was watching a tennis match, looking back and forth as they presented their reasonable arguments. In an effort to help the situation, I was forced to reach into the depths of my mental toolbox ideas, helpful hints, compromising techniques, and whatever else I could make up to ease the tension. On the verge of my own failure, I asked the wife why she was so adamant about getting rid of the box. She replied simply that it was of no value or use. So, I asked her in return for some perspective: "What if your husband believed your diamonds were no longer of value and should be sold?" This clearly hit a nerve, creating a silence in the room as they both absorbed the truthfulness of the different views. Unfortunately, this is reality. In this case, the tennis match ended with a pretty good chuckle, but the wife won, and I carried the box to the trash for them.

As you take your first pass at the closet or room, remember to use the thinning technique, removing the items that no longer capture the emotional connection you're longing to preserve. Why keep an item that you were never fond of, carries no emotional connection, or conjures up a negative reaction? While it would be wonderful if your home was large enough for you to keep everything, we know that's impossible in most cases. Regardless of how neat and organized we are, the quantity of belongings we collect over the years is astonishing. Why is it that most people have a large collection of T-shirts? You know the ones – shirts that are purchased on vacations, represent your school or favorite sports team, symbolize an athletic event, or that you just think are cool. I have entered homes were the T-shirt collection is folded perfectly on the shelves of a closet just waiting to be sorted. This is a great place to start, as you can eliminate 30 percent of the shirts in the first twenty minutes of the project just by thinning out the ones that have less meaning. Take the time to reminisce about the T-shirt's story before placing it in the SHARE or DONATE PILES. You have now successfully reduced the large pile of shirts to a manageable collection.

The items in the KEEP PILE will always carry sentimental value, offering a special connection to you, your loved one, and your ancestors. Over the years, these sacred items might be repurposed or eventually end up in a different pile; for now, though, they will remain in the KEEP PILE.

PILE #2 – SHARE

The SHARE PILE comprises items you would like to share with friends and family members. Whether the items are honoring a person after they passed or are family heirlooms to be shared with the next generation, this pile expresses a willingness to interject a part of your history with others. From the griever's perspective, the sharing of items is a loving gesture, the true act of bestowing a memory on the receiver who accepts such an extraordinary gift.

To this day, I can still visualize Rod's running buddy's face when I presented him with the bright yellow watch. He accepted this gesture with such pride and honor knowing he was tasked with carrying on Rod's legacy. As with Rod's bicycle, I get great pleasure participating in triathlons with Rod's brother, watching his blue Stella fly by. There is no question that I would have preferred Rod to be with us physically in our athletic endeavors, but I was satisfied having a piece of him with me in the same event.

As you've worked on your game plan to sort through the closets, you've likely identified people with whom you'd like to share items, and the time has now come to determine who gets what. You've identified many items in advance and placed them in in your SHARE PILE or otherwise marked them for sharing. As you move right to left/left to right in each room, be sure to mark the item with the recipient's name using a sticky note, label, or other form of identifier. Once completed, update your two lists. It's okay to not have a recipient for everything yet. It will come to you when the time is right.

Throughout the years, I have found that a truly comforting, uplifting, and soothing gesture is to personalize items for the recipients by attaching a message to it using a label or permanent marker before presenting it.

Here are a few of ideas to try when sharing items:

- **Sharing ties or scarves:** An endearing way to share a tie or scarf is to adhere a cloth label with a name, quote, or special message sewn on the backside of a tie or the side of a scarf. Writing special notes in Rod's ties became a wonderful therapeutic project for me; I found pleasure in matching a particular tie with a special person based on color, style, and the history of the tie. The most rewarding part of the project was sharing his ties with his friends, colleagues, and family. I witnessed the tears of joy and knew in my heart they missed Rod as much as I did.

- **Sharing books:** Before you share any books, print labels with a name, quote, personal message, or whatever feels right to be affixed to the inside cover. Who gets which book would be based on the recipient's love of a specific genre or memory shared together. If you have traveled with someone in the past, possibly share a travel book with them. If you have a specific coffee table book a recipient can connect with, be sure to write your special note about why you chose that book for them. A short time ago, I was assisting a woman pack her books as she prepared for a move to an assisted-living home. I had suggested to her on a previous visit the idea of placing labels in the books before she gave them away. As we pulled the books off the shelves, assigning them to the appropriate person, she wrote a lovely note. We spent the entire afternoon matching people to specific books, and she especially found great pride in sharing her favorite books with her grandchildren.

- **Sharing ball caps:** Similar to labeling the ties, lay the assortment of ball caps you would like to share on a bed or countertop. Take the time to match the hat with a person, using a Sharpie to write a special note on the underside of the hat's bill. I can pretty much guarantee when the hat is received, it will become the recipient's new favorite.

Clothing and jewelry are often the more straightforward items to give away. In many cases, there is an association or relationship between the piece of jewelry and its recipient. Or maybe in your heart you know exactly who should receive what. Following clothing and jewelry, the next grouping is sports equipment or hobby paraphernalia. If your loved one played Mahjongg with a group of women each week, you may want to share her case of tiles with a special friend in the group. If she was a member of a knitting club, a club mate would be honored to knit with her needles. Just as I shared Rod's bicycle, the same can occur with golf clubs, fishing rods, and tennis rackets. If possible, personalize the item with a special note, sticker, or marking.

A friend shared her personal story with me of when she was moving from California to Colorado. Just before she left, her best friend had lost her battle with cancer, leaving behind a two-year-old daughter. When my friend was saying good-bye to the little girl and her father, he suggested sharing his wife's winter coat with her to keep warm in Colorado. That coat has created an incredible bond between two friends in both life and death; my friend wears the coat during the cooler months. On a recent trip back to California, the little girl recognized the coat, sharing, "That is my mommy's coat." It is the simple touches and gestures that provide happiness and connection when sharing personal possessions.

Another category of shareable possessions is accumulated airline miles and hotel points for future travel. These items can be used to plan a special trip together, maybe a trip for a grandchild to visit a grandparent, or a trip for a sibling to visit their brother at college. The sharing of accrued airline miles has tremendous benefits, both financial and emotional. Recently, I was on a trip where I met a widow who was traveling the world using her husband's accrued frequent flyer miles. She was determined to visit all the places on his bucket list that he was unable to visit before his untimely death. On this particular trip, she was traveling with her sister, and using his miles provided a rewarding and terrific experience for both.

In Chapter 5, "Being Prepared, Managing Your Possessions, Creating the Lifestyle," I will share examples of how to document, earmark, and prepare for the distribution of items before a death occurs. I encourage all my clients to create a plan in advance in order to set expectations of what to do with personal belongings. In creating a plan, you can avoid family disappointment or surprises, as the documents can be part of your will and/or trust.

PILE #3 – DONATE

The DONATE PILE is also known as the "feel-good pile," as it can give you comfort knowing that your or a loved one's belongings will support others who are in need. In many cases, the items will have a direct benefit to an individual, or they may be used to help raise funds for a specific cause through a retail resale arrangement. Whatever the case, others will benefit from your donation, making this a great way to honor yourself or a loved one.

There are a variety of local and national agencies that accept all types of donations, while others specialize in particular items such as shoes, in-home medical supplies, or household goods. When placing items in your DONATE PILE, I recommend sorting them into smaller groupings of similar items to ensure a match with the appropriate donation agency. For instance, your subpiles can be identified as women's clothing, men's clothing, shoes, household items, in-home medical supplies, children's toys, or furniture. Or, if it is easier for you, just add all your donated items to one pile and task a team member to sort the items into subgroups and have them drop off the items at the associated agencies.

When working with individuals, I use this approach to ensure donations are made to agencies that match with a mission they're passionate about. There is nothing more gratifying than helping raise funds for a program you are passionately connected to; for example, in support of a family member's health challenge. During a recent project, my client was adamant about donating her husband's belongings to veterans, as she had a passion for helping those who have served our country. Once she created her DONATE PILE, we placed all the items in bags, reached out to the Vietnam Veterans of America program to arrange a pickup, and the bags were gone the next day. Truly a feel-good donation.

There are so many wonderful agencies in need of donations, you can probably find one with a mission that best fits your passions. The most popular agencies for donations are those associated with religious affiliations, third-world advocacy, health initiatives, or underserved children.

A sampling of donation subgroups:

- **General clothing and household donations:**
  These items are accepted by a variety of local and national agencies. Many offer pickup

services, tax donations, and a storefront to resell the items. These agencies will accept most household items, including furniture. A brief list: Salvation Army, Goodwill Industries, Boys & Girls Clubs of America, Arc Thrift Stores, Vietnam Veterans of America. In addition, many communities have locally owned thrift and resale shops. You can find more resources online.

- **Work clothing donations:** These agencies accept donations in support of promoting career changes, job searches, and reentry into the workplace. In most cases, they prefer up-to-date styles that have been cleaned, pressed, and are acceptable for the workplace. This is a very useful way to donate suits, ties, slacks, dresses, skirts, and blouses. A few examples include Dress for Success and Balance Careers, both of whom specialize in career planning.

- **Shoe donations:** There are a variety of agencies that specialize in shoe donations. Specifically, I recommend donating business-appropriate shoes as part of work-clothing donations and donating sneakers to a running store to be sent to developing countries. The not-for-profit agency Soles4souls has distributed 35 million pairs of shoes to those in need, and they will accept all shoes.

- **Warm clothing/winter coats:** Warm clothing is always needed in the northern states to support people experiencing homelessness or underserved children. Many dry cleaners sponsor a fall coat drive each year, often with a donation box in the store entrance for easy access. In addition, many houses of worship collect warm clothing to distribute to their constituents and share with less fortunate populations.

- **In-home medical supplies:** If you were a family caregiver, your home may have incorporated a hospital bed, a cane, a walker, and an array of medical supplies. These items, while extremely useful to share with others, do have guidelines for donations. However, not all agencies will accept health-related items, so I recommend contacting your local hospice or a not-for-profit such as Project Cure who accepts donations to distribute outside the United States.

Not everyone knows immediately who they would like to donate their belongings to or even if they are ready to donate. It's perfectly acceptable for these ideas to percolate over time, allowing you to figure out the best fit for your belongings. As I described, it took thirteen years to donate my daughter's crib. I hadn't ever intended to donate it, but eventually the idea was triggered because of a relationship I had with an agency whose mission was important.

Fortunately, I am exposed to many marvelous stories of the impact donations have had on both donor and recipient. For example, a young widow whose husband died in an accident chose to take her husband's shoes to an impoverished village in Mexico to donate to the local villagers. One pair of his surplus shoes became someone else's only shoes. The experience for her was powerful, and the villagers now had footwear. Another widow donated her husband's collection of professional sports memorabilia to a fund-raiser for a grief and loss center. She had been wrestling with the best fit for the items because she was not a sports fan herself, and the fund-raiser provided the perfect outlet for her husband's collection. A family who lost their eldest son donated his collection of musical instruments to an after-school music program. A woman downsizing her home donated wall art to an area hospice to improve the ambiance in the lobby.

The DONATE PILE really is the feel-good pile, and as a bonus, in most cases your donation is tax deductible.

PILE #4 – SELL

Your SELL PILE represents items of monetary value that are salable – items you have chosen not to keep for yourself or share with others. Why not create an income stream with your items? You can use the funds to pay bills, create a lasting memorial, embark on an adventure, or just save the proceeds for a rainy day.

Just as there is no timeline when starting to sort through closets, there is no timeline for selling the items. The goal is to identify what you would like to sell and later determine the best approach for making the sale. When you are ready, engage one of your expert team members, a family member, the special friend itching to help you in some way, or go online yourself and start researching.

When your sell pile is complete, it's time to prepare your items for their "photo shoot." You can bring new life to an item simply by dusting, repairing scratches, or washing it. When items are ready, stage them to look their best by ensuring the lighting is just right, they sit on or in front of a solid surface, and they are positioned in a way to capture the best angle. These pictures serve as the first impression when capturing a potential buyer. Whether you plan on selling the item electronically, via consignment, or in person, having digital or printed photographs will assist in the sale.

Before you choose the best approach, make a list of which items you're planning to sell, the dollar amount you believe each item will sell for (and then reduce it by 20 percent), the method of sale (listed below), and who the potential buyer would be; for example, an individual versus an agency. Using this tactic, you will manage expectations and identify your target audience. And always remember, a potential buyer will perceive the worth of the item differently than you do. After all, they are purchasing a secondhand item, and unless it is a collector's item such as art or jewelry, the buyer can set the value.

How do you choose the most effective way to sell each item? That will vary based on where you live and how internet savvy either you or your helper is. When selling on the internet, your physical location doesn't matter as much (unless you're selling large items such as furniture), as the item can be shipped to the purchaser.

Approaches for selling items:

- **National websites:** Of all the websites available to sell personal belongings, the most popular place is eBay. This site allows you to set preferences for each item, allowing them to be sold at either a flat-rate price or in a bidding auction that is live until a designated date. Once an item has a buyer, it is your responsibility to ship it to the purchaser. In some cases, I have found that selling items on eBay is a great project for children or grandchildren, as they are most likely computer savvy, will be creative with their descriptions, and can prepare the item for shipping with very little hassle.

  Another popular site is Etsy, where all items are listed at a flat-rate price.

- **Local websites:** Similar to national sites, a local website can be helpful in selling items in your neighborhood or metropolitan area. Websites such as Craigslist do have a national presence; however, you can post your item locally for sale. A few hints when using Craigslist: research similar items to help price the item appropriately, create an enticing subject line describing the item, refresh often so the item will be moved to the top, drop the price after a few days, and most importantly, when delivering the item meet the person in a public place for safety reasons. I have found grocery store parking lots to be a great place to exchange money for the item.

Other sites to consider include LetGo and OfferUp; Facebook also has local marketplaces where you can sell your items.

All of these sites all have apps that you can download to your smartphone, making the process even simpler – either for you, or for your more tech-savvy friends and family to help you with.

- **Garage/Yard Sale:** A garage or yard sale work best when you have a large array of items and simply don't want to deal with online sales. If this approach works for you, there are many ways to attract people to your sale. You can advertise online, on local news sites, and/or place signs off main streets with specific directions to your sale. You can also invite your neighbors to participate with their own garage sale or add to yours, bringing additional foot traffic. The key to the sale is pricing and negotiating. Set reasonable prices, be willing to negotiate, and have lots of small change on hand.

- **Consignment Sale:** The most practical items to sell via a consignment arrangement are sports equipment, furniture, jewelry, and expensive or designer clothing. Most communities have at least one store that sells consignment merchandise; many have more. To locate one near you, a quick online search is your best bet. The arrangements vary based on the owner of the store; however, the standard protocol is that you provide the items to the store, the store arranges for the sale, and when the item is sold, you are paid a percentage of the sale price.

- **Creative Individual Sales:** This approach is best when you create your own captured audience based on the items you are selling. For example, if you have art to sell you might reach out to art dealers, or if you have a collection of fishing equipment you can reach out to a fishing club. One widow was very resourceful selling her husband's motorized athletic equipment via a personal auction. When he passed, she became responsible for his many snowmobiles, motorcycles, trailers, tools, sports equipment, and more. She hired an auctioneer and sold each item to the highest bidder.

Whichever approach or combination of approaches works best for you, always remember your monetary value of an item is not the same as the buyer's. Success is based on selling the item for a reasonable price and feeling good about the sale. If a particular item is not selling, lower the price or consider donating it.

PILE #5 – DISPOSE

The DISPOSE PILE is the most straightforward of all the piles. It consists of items being sent to a landfill or recycling plant. As you sort through drawers, closets, garages, and basements, the items that don't have any value to you, to someone else, or are simply not salable should be discarded via trash or recycling.

Because the majority of physical items will fit into one of the other five piles, the DISPOSE PILE consists mostly of paper items. Even though we are moving toward a paperless world, many people still have filing cabinets and drawers filled with old tax returns, bank statements, and medical records. And oftentimes we don't remember where we filed anything, making most of it superfluous. So it's time to thin, shred, scan, and recycle paper. And personally, I believe it's easier to access electronic files, so why not scan documents, photographs, and all the rest to create an electronic filing system?

A word of caution: when sorting through paper items, be sure to look in envelopes for hidden cash, stock certificates, birth certificates, or other legal documents that require you to keep a paper copy. And how fun would it be to find a beautiful love letter, a special recognition or award, a newspaper clipping, or a poem?

As you place items in the DISPOSE PILE, keep in mind that what you might think is trash others might see as perfect for an art project, Halloween costume, decoration, or school-supply box. In other words, don't throw away, for example, buttons, hangers, gift boxes, binders, office supplies, or anything that can be upcycled or recycled. Believe it or not, people collect old magazines, tin canisters, and other vintage items. These items can be donated to an agency that collects household donations or to an art department at a nearby school.

Here are a few tricks to keep in mind when organizing your DISPOSE FILE:

- **Shred sensitive documents:** In today's crazy world, prevent identity theft by shredding old tax returns, bank statements, and other documents containing personal data. If you don't own a shredder, office supply stores shred at a reasonable cost, or search for a community safety drive offering free shredding on a particular day.

- **Managing your recycling:** Before you recycle, empty paper from notebooks, remove paper clips and staples, and pile papers so they take up as little room as possible. If you are recycling cardboard, be sure to break down the boxes to save space. A true faux pas of recycling is to mix it with trash, so be sure to keep the piles separate.

As you sort each item into either trash or recycling, ask yourself if anyone else can use it before making a final decision.

PILE #6 – PONDER

The PONDER PILE is the most important in the Magic of Six Piles. The purpose of the PONDER PILE is to have a place for any item whose fate you have pondered for more than two or three minutes. If you ponder for too long, there is the potential for you to derail the project or lose your momentum as you try to make a difficult decision. Why make a final decision if you don't have to? This pile can be revisited in the future, so use the PONDER PILE and do your best to keep the project on track.

Belongings that land in the PONDER PILE might include a few clothing items, photographs (more on this in Chapter 4), wallets and their contents, papers from the home office, family heirlooms that you may not be interested in keeping, electronics (see Chapter 4), and meaningful trinkets. Some of the items in my Rod pile are things that might wind up in a PONDER PILE – items that aren't actually useful to you or anyone else, yet you still have an attachment to them. In my case, I saved many of these items and am so thankful I did, as they hold many memories and tell Rod's story.

The best way to manage your PONDER PILE is to place everything in a box, label it "PONDER PILE," and set a date for revisiting it. Although the date might slip, at least you are setting a goal to reexamine the contents. And if you need a bit of encouragement when you're ready to revisit, engage a special friend or family member to help. The items in the box could become a permanent keep box or a future memorial box.

The Magic of Six Piles techniques have proven to be very successful in identifying the best place for items as you sort. Whether you are cleaning out or simply thinning the items in a room, the process will work the same. Think of it as playing a game: all you have to do is follow a routine of working right to left/left to right, placing each item in one of six piles. Once you've placed items in one of the six piles, you, or you and your team, can get your items where they need to be.

CHAPTER 4

WHEN CIRCUMSTANCES ARE NOT STRAIGHTFORWARD

When sorting or thinning personal belongings, the process for the most part is straightforward. Although you may get hung up on a few items here and there, they'll quickly find their way to the PONDER PILE where you can revisit them in the future. By now, you, or you and your team, have found a great cadence, you have reminisced with your loved one as you touched each item, you have helped others by donating the items that you no longer need, and most importantly, you feel empowered by knowing that you can complete the effort you started.

While the six piles create a great framework for sorting through closets, drawers, and cabinets, there are often certain situations that need additional introspection. What happens with possessions that require more understanding or negotiation with others? For example, what do you do with collections? Do you keep the collection together, or is it okay to break it up, sharing the items with several people or selling them individually? What about the hundreds of photographs you have in print or digital files? Do you keep them all, or do you dispose of some? But most importantly, how do you decide? And the most frequently asked question I hear now is what to do with digital assets – electronic files, mobile applications, and social media accounts. These are just a few examples of the kinds of circumstances that can require more patience, planning, and compromise than the six piles can support.

COLLECTIONS

In all my years of providing support, I have yet to meet an individual or family who doesn't collect something. And while you may think you don't collect, you probably do. Collections can include kitchen gadgets, stuffed animals, yard ornaments, travel memorabilia, stamps, baseball cards, and holiday decor, just to name a few. Maybe the collection began with one item that caught your eye, and over time you've added additional pieces as they've brought you more joy, or your passion increased. You get the picture. So when you come across a loved one's collection, how do you determine whether to break it up or keep it together? Start by asking yourself whether there is more impact or meaning if the objects remain together, or can the pieces stand on their own?

Over the years, I have had my own share of collections that I questioned. The one I continue to hold on to is my tractor collection, a concept that, thanks to my friends and family, emerged after Rod passed away. Like most collections, this one also has a backstory. I had only been in Kansas City for ten months when Rod passed, having just moved from Washington, D.C. We were making our way back to Colorado, where we wanted to raise our daughter, when suddenly I found myself in the nation's breadbasket – blessed with miles and miles of fertile farmland, but no family roots or personal connection to the region after growing up in New England. I repeated over and over to those closest to me that I could not believe Rod left me in the Midwest, so people started memorializing my predicament by giving me all types of tractors – toys, collectibles, books, tractor-themed gadgets. Although the ensuing tractor collection represented a very difficult time in my life, I couldn't bear the thought of breaking it up.

So how do you decide whether to keep collections intact or break them up? The answer is mostly subjective. As I said earlier, if you believe all the pieces should remain together, then the collection needs to remain together, at least until you decide otherwise. If the collection retains its value only as a full collection, then you'll probably want to keep it together. But individual items of a collection – for example stamps or coins – can have value as stand-alone items, too. To compare the monetary value of a collection versus individual items, take advantage of online resources. There are plenty of websites that can help you at least start the process of valuing your collection or item. And if you want to sell an item, remember that the realistic appraisal value is what you should expect to receive, not your own perception of the value.

If the collection does contain some monetary value or historical significance – such as a fine art collection, antiques, or pop culture memorabilia – then it could be worthwhile to bring in an expert to assess its value, or guide you in splitting it up if that's what you choose. An expert would be able to determine if all or some objects in the collection would be best remaining together, while others could be split up. Perhaps there are clear divides within the collection that help you decide which items you'd like to keep, while clearing out others.

If money is not a factor, then deciding what to do with a collection can be even less clear. In this case, one strategy for thinning a collection is to mimic how a museum exhibition is handled. Pretend you are tasked with creating a curated exhibition of the collection at hand. As with curators at a museum, you must first determine the story you want to tell and then find the pieces that best support your message. In this case, what are the highlights of the collection? Which individual pieces evoke the most emotion or memories? Can you eliminate duplicate pieces or pick one that exemplifies a subset of the collection? With a museum collection, there are many painting and objects that ultimately never see the light of the gallery. They are either too small, too similar to a superior example, or maybe not in good enough condition to share with the public. Look at your collection through a similar lens, and you'll be surprised at how much easier it will be to make these tough decisions.

My mother's Hummel Figurine collection is good example of how a debate can occur when trying to decide what is best for a collection, especially when others are involved. My sisters and I had to ask ourselves whether we would keep her Hummels together as a collection or divide it into five groups, one for each daughter. How do we choose between monetary and emotional value? Would it be better for each of us to have a piece in memory of our mother, or would we find it more valuable to sell it to a collector? My main point here is that the answer is not straightforward and should be open for discussion. And what about the family that can't decide? Do you compromise or do you take a vote? Since not everyone will be satisfied with the outcome, what are you willing to compromise on? These questions are often best answered before you even begin. As I mentioned in Chapter 3, as you prepare to tackle a collection, be mindful of everyone's hopes, fears, and ideal outcomes. Using the example of the figurines, let's say that several of us are happy to sell them to an avid collector, while others feel offended at the idea because of how much they meant to our mother. In this case, I would suggest the following course of action. First, it would be worthwhile to bring in an expert to assess the collection's monetary value so that you have some facts on what a potential sale would entail and how much the collection is worth. I would then propose sorting and ranking the figurines before making any final decisions. Are there pieces that are particularly emotional, valuable, or wanted by a certain sister? Once we address the collection objectively, it's time to propose some options and make some compromises. Depending on how big the collection is, would it be satisfactory for each sister to pick two or three pieces they connect to and can easily incorporate into their own home, then sell or donate the rest? Does the collection's monetary value change anyone's opinion? Would it be possible to sell some of the collection and donate the money to a relevant cause? Proposing multiple options can help the group feel collaborative and possibly reduce any tension or hurt feelings. It can also make the process a bit more rewarding if you are able to incorporate a piece of every party's vision.

In another moment of compromise, a couple who were recently emptying their house for an upcoming move were confronted with the husband's collection of hunting trophies. The wife was adamant that she did not want them in their new home, yet her husband wanted to take them all with him as keepsakes and a show of his accomplishments in his chosen hobby. Through some research, we learned that taxidermy professionals often purchase trophies for resale at a reasonable price, which provided the wife with an option for compromising on a collection she felt was simply too large. Since breaking up the collection had no bearing on the overall value, I suggested to the husband that he keep his favorites and sell the rest to satisfy his wife and to make some extra money.

What about pieces that were acquired at a time when they were not considered collector's items, but now are? For example, when my daughter was young, she amassed a sizable number of TY Beanie Babies. Nowadays, they can truly be a collection and a great memory for the children and parents who collected them. Would it be best to save them as the collection or break them up? If you visit eBay, Beanie Babies are being sold individually with prices based on availability. In the case of my daughter's collection, we chose to focus on the collection's future purpose. While my daughter is grown and has long been gone from the house, we find that our littlest visitors still love these charming animals. I can't even count how many times they have been brought out to build a zoo and entertain a toddler. In our case, we chose to keep the collection, since the next generation loves learning about the different animals. The purpose of our collection is largely the same, but it has since found a new audience to appreciate its collective nature.

When addressing collections, it's important to look at the facts before making any decisions. If you're able to objectively evaluate the collection ahead of time, then the right decision or options will essentially present themselves. In summary, things to consider include size, relationship of objects, monetary value, emotional value, and future value. Are any of these a fixed variable that needs to be addressed? For example, you need to reduce the size because of space limitations, or you need to sell something for the extra income. And for unfixed variables, which outcome is more important to you? Does it bring you more peace to keep as much of the collection together as possible, or is it more important to see a new life emerge for the objects? If you are able to define and prioritize these areas of information, then the solution can be more straightforward, and you will more quickly find peace in the process.

PHOTOGRAPHS

Photographs are an interesting challenge today as technology continues to advance. For many of us, our photos are primarily stored on our devices or in the cloud and are almost always accessible one way or another. However, this doesn't mean there aren't myriad ways photographs are stored, something important to keep in mind as you start thinking about sorting through them. They are often hanging on walls, displayed in frames in every room, housed in photo albums, stored in electronic files, or piled in boxes. It can feel overwhelming. Where do you begin? What do you save? And in what format? What do you do with the endless boxes of printed photos, negatives, photo albums, slides, and picture frames? There are so many wonderful moments captured in these pictures, and there is certainly something nostalgic about holding a printed photograph as opposed to looking at one on a screen. While sorting photographs can seem a daunting task, I have actually observed the opposite when helping people. The memories a picture can provide are priceless, especially as time goes by. We are often most drawn to the simple observations captured in the photograph: the house before it had trees, the decade's style of clothing, the cars, the vacations, the speed at which time flies by as children grow up. Pictures embody the stories of people's lives and the places they have been.

The primary challenge is coming up with game plan for how to sort, thin, and store the photos. Before the age of digital media, photos and their accompanying negatives had to be physically stored somewhere. Some people resorted to simply filling shoebox after shoebox, while others were a bit more organized and created photo albums, usually in sequential order. Since we now capture thousands of pictures with our mobile phones and digital cameras, storing photos has significantly changed – to the delight of some and the consternation of others. How do you manage the collection of images, and what is the best approach for sorting through the pictures when someone passes away or when you are downsizing a home?

In my experience, the best way to organize photos is to create a plan that allows enough time to reminisce, sort, thin, and then store them. Start by creating an environment that is comfortable and relaxing – a snowy or rainy weekend, favorite background music, snacks, a bottle of wine, your favorite loungewear – whatever feels right for you.

Before you open your first box or log on to your device, determine what method you would like to use to organize, share, and save your photographs.

Here are a few suggestions:

- **Design a digital filing system:** The most popular method for storing pictures is in digital format. Whether the pictures are stored on your hard drive or in the cloud, choosing a filing system will provide you easy access. I suggest labeling your pictures with a date, location, name(s), and event for easier sorting and retrieval. Once you have created your filing system, move your photos to the appropriate folders. Make sure to scan your physical photographs and file these as well. For ongoing maintenance, I suggest revisiting files to thin out pictures of less importance. Do you really need to save three thousand pictures from your trip to Italy?

- **Create themed photo albums:** While this might sound tedious, the process is actually fun and a great way to store pictures. With today's online resources, photo albums are easy and fun to create. Some families create a book for each year that include key highlights, while others create books capturing a vacation, sports season, home renovation, family reunion, and other milestones. These books are easy to create, even for those who don't consider themselves crafty, and with a few clicks, you can have them delivered to your home.

- **Create a storybook of your or your loved one's journey through life:** Starting at birth, tell the story of where they lived, aspects of their childhood, college experiences, young adult life, building a family, and other significant adventures they experienced. While you are sorting through the pictures, create a digital or physical pile of those you'd like include. Be sure to tell the story with both words and pictures. When you're ready, scan physical or collect digital photos for the story, and create a book online to be printed. You can make several copies to provide to friends and family members.

- **Create a "Wall of Fame":** As you sort through the photos, set aside those that capture important milestones and would make a vibrant gallery wall that captures the happiest memories. In my wall of fame, for example, we have photos of weddings, family, childhood, athletic events, graduations, and other significant milestones. We love when people ask questions about specific pictures, allowing us to share the story.

- **Update pictures in frames:** When is the last time you changed a photograph in a picture frame? Fifteen years ago, you placed your favorite picture of your children in a frame, and you haven't replaced it since. The original can still be a favorite, but by updating the photo, the frame may no longer look dated, and you'll have a new picture to enjoy.

Whenever I change a picture, I like to keep the past pictures inside the frame behind the current one. It is a wonderful experience flipping through them the next time you update the frame. And as you change out photos, you can also move them around. That school photo in the living room from fifteen years ago would be a great addition to the wall of fame – the perfect designated place for a blend of past and present.

You are now ready to open the first box or digital file and sort through the pictures. Remember to use the same techniques you used with your personal belongings. Start by thinning the photos, tossing those that have scenery or people that are no longer relevant. Using a similar approach to the Magic of Six Piles, you can keep, share, scan, toss, ponder, or inquire. If there's someone else who might know the history of the photograph, consider asking for their help. Work through one pile, box, or digital folder at a time, and maintain your cadence. While the process can be tedious, the experience is rewarding and fulfilling, as there is nothing better than learning or reminiscing about the history of a loved one.

DIGITAL POSSESSIONS

Similar to photographs, other digital data has introduced a new category of possessions, presenting sorting challenges that we haven't yet collectively solved – especially since technology and software evolve so quickly. What happens to hardware, software, stored data, and social media content when someone passes away or is no longer capable of maintaining their devices? While it can feel overwhelming at first, other than scrambling for passwords, the process is similar to sorting through closets, home offices, and boxes of miscellaneous items. The real difference is that the amount of material to sort through is immense and often monotonous, as the majority of users rarely delete files.

What might be popular today may become obsolete tomorrow, so I'll share general strategies for digital possessions rather than platform-specific ones. Similar to organizing a closet or drawer, individuals use and organize data within electronic devices differently. If you need help with this set of possessions, make sure you find someone who is computer savvy. This will help accelerate the process and eliminate frustrations.

Following are five key areas relating to digital possessions and associated approaches for reconciling hardware, related data, and social media content:

- **Passwords:** If you're dealing with a loved one who passed, hopefully they left you an organized list of all online accounts and associated passwords. Unfortunately, this is usually not the case. There might be a partial list somewhere; however, many passwords change frequently, and most people fail to update the list – if they had one to begin with. Your first challenge, though, may be finding the password to access the device itself. If you're lucky, you'll have a list of these passwords to refer to. If you don't, consider consulting with a professional to see if you have any options or there are any workarounds.

Assuming you're able to access the device, start with a list of accounts you're trying to access, and methodically work through them one at a time, changing user names and passwords. A short list of accounts would include banking, utilities, social media, membership organizations, credit cards, and retail accounts. If you have trouble accessing accounts, you may find that your loved one has saved their passwords on their device, which will automatically enter them when prompted. Sometimes, you can simply click on "forgot password" and create a new one. Many companies have strict security measures in place, however, and if this is the case, you may have to share a death certificate with the relevant institution to obtain access to the account. I suggest asking for assistance from someone you trust, as the process can be time-consuming and frustrating. Be patient, as security is important and most companies have policies and procedures that the customer service agent must follow.

- **Voicemail:** Hearing the voice of your loved one on their voicemail message is a prized digital possession. I have witnessed people call their loved one's phone over and over again just to hear their voice one more time. I have also observed individuals saving a cell phone for years so they can continue to call and listen to their voice. But, as we know, maintaining a cell phone account is expensive. You do, however, have other options. There are software products available to save the message in an MP3 or other file format, allowing you to download it onto your own device where it's ready for you any time you want to hear it.

- **Data:** The largest portion of digital possessions is the data stored as documents, pictures, spreadsheets, emails, lists, contacts, calendars, and so on. What of this do you want to save, and what should be deleted? The rule of thumb is if no one has opened a file in years, there is no reason to open it now. While you might find something of interest in it, there are so many other files that it really makes sense to stick to the more recent data. Similar to sorting through photographs, create a process that works for you. Start with thinning out the files by deleting as many as you can. In my opinion, the most important data is contacts, account information, and anything that is fairly current.

It is also okay to keep some files that you find endearing or show your loved one's passions. Do they have a list of books or movies they wanted to see? Or maybe they had a log of working out or tasks associated with a hobby. Those will be fun to return to at a later date, complete for them, or share with family and friends.

- **Social Media:** Social media is a tough and complicated area, and there are many strong opinions both for and against keeping an account open after someone passes. I would suggest relying first on your knowledge of your loved one, and focus on what you believe *they* would have wanted. Then add your own opinion as well as family members' thoughts where relevant. How connected was your loved one to their social media accounts? Were they regular users, or did they simply use the accounts to look at other people's content? Did they ever comment on or share an opinion in a similar situation? All of these questions can help you think about what they would have wanted.

  I have talked extensively thus far on the importance of creating a personal story, and social networks are the most curated and public displays of one's life. With that in mind, it is important to honor this aspect of someone's life. But the big question is, do you do it publicly or privately? With Facebook, for example, I have often seen people continue to comment on a deceased person's page on their birthday, death day, or just in moments of intense longing. For some, this is a beautiful display of grief and serves as a public memorial, while for others it can feel inappropriate or invasive. As the living, we do deserve some latitude, but it is a personal call whether you would like to see this continued activity. With Instagram, for example, the nature of engagement is different, and there is less continued activity if a user isn't actively posting. Again, whether you would like your loved one's followers to be able to continue accessing the content or posting comments is a personal discussion/ decision.

Logistically, there are certain procedures for maintaining a social media account that vary based on the platform and their security measures. The unwritten rule associated with a social media account is that the account is owned and maintained by the person who activated it. But when a death has occurred, many loved ones will deactivate the accounts or at least change the preferences to prevent people from adding comments. But some companies, such as Facebook, have been revisiting their policies, permitting a user to set up a legacy account or set preferences in the event of their death, making it much easier work with.

Whatever you choose, I would also suggest saving as much content as you feel relevant. Capturing screenshots of past Facebook and Twitter posts and saving Instagram photos with the captions is a great way to memorialize a loved one and truly capture their voice and view of the world. You can always make another photo album of this content to look at during years to come, or create a memorial or wall of fame specifically with framed social media photos. And if you'd like to keep an account in its entirety without keeping it live, it's also possible to download entire archives of some accounts (you can search online for instructions on how to do this).

- **Hardware/Devices:** The disposing, reallocating, or selling of hardware when sorting through possessions is no different from someone replacing their hardware with a newer version. For safety purposes, be sure to clear the data and recycle the hardware as you may have done in the past.

With the addition of digital possessions to the collection, the twenty-first century has created a new dimension of possessions. The most important takeaway here is to get your affairs in order as best you can if possible, and to encourage loved ones to do the same. And as you sort through a loved one's digital possessions, think of what it would be like for someone else to have to sort through yours. Finally, when you have completed this project, take a break – and then organize your own data!

UNEXPECTED DISCOVERIES

Sorting through someone else's belongings can be rewarding and comforting, but what happens when you discover something you were not expecting? Whether the discovery is heartening or hurtful, good or bad, exciting or upsetting, it is a discovery that can trigger an emotional reaction or cause havoc.

Let's start with the good. When I recently helped a friend sort through her family's personal belongings, we discovered an assortment of treasures including cash, gift cards (some had expired), a long-lost earring, pictures from her childhood, and a few cards she had received from her children. My friend was ecstatic about her findings, especially since her mother had given her the pair of earrings when she got married. In this case, these discoveries changed her outlook on the whole process of cleaning, and gave her renewed energy to keep going. Another positive story a colleague shared with me was finding several diaries when she cleared the home of a friend who had passed away. My colleague was genuinely torn about how to handle the situation, wanting to honor the privacy of her friend. As diaries are so personal, she felt she was not the right person to destroy a lifetime of intimate entries. In the end, she gave the diaries to her friend's family in the hope that they would destroy them without reading the pages, and they did. The secrets were kept confidential.

While both of those stories are heartwarming, what happens when you discover a dreaded item or situation you thought you would never find? One family member learned her finances were different from what she believed them to be. Her husband had gambled their savings and cashed in a life insurance policy to pay off his debt. Or what if you discover your loved one wasn't faithful, or you learn about a transgression that you might have suspected yet never confronted. The most hurtful part of these stories is that you cannot confront the person to ask why; you can only work through the pain. I share these stories with you in preparation for what you might find. Unfortunately, not everyone has a positive experience when sorting through drawers, cabinets, and closets.

When I was presenting at a conference a few years ago, a widow in the audience shared with the group that she had found of a locked military box in her husband's closet following his sudden death. For two years, she wondered what the contents of the box could be. She never shared the discovery with friends or family as she was frightened that the contents might change the impression they had of her husband. Over the years, she wondered if the metal box contained something personal that would be hurtful, or maybe it was ammunition or a gun, or maybe it was even empty. Her fears prevented her from opening the box, and she had never told anyone until she attended the conference. A gentleman in the audience offered to be with her when she opened it. Although he was a stranger, he was also in the process of sorting his wife's personal possessions, and could provide support and understanding that would be different from that of friends and family. When opening the box together, they found local currency from countries he had been deployed to during his military career.

Over the years, I have heard both amazingly wonderful and heart-wrenching stories of unexpected discoveries. My only true advice is if you find something that you fear might be upsetting, find someone you trust to be with you when you open the envelope or reach in the box. Keep in mind that you don't have to decide right away – you're entitled to set something aside in your PONDER PILE. And if you'd rather not share at all, you can tuck an unexpected item back into a drawer or box. And remember, you get to choose if you even want to look.

RESENTMENT

Resentment can be tricky to manage, either on your own or with a close friend, because it is often a mixture of anger, fear, and disappointment. And any of these emotions can rear its head at any given time, making it difficult to think and act rationally. This type of emotional response can arise as the result of many situations, but it often follows a family disagreement after the death of a parent, relocation of a parent to an assisted-living arrangement, or when there is a death by suicide. In these situations, the resentment will likely cause a delay in sorting through personal possessions.

Many family lawyers and counselors will attest that when someone has not set their affairs in order prior to a death, the outcome can become devastating for individual family members. Each surviving family member has a personal opinion about the best approach for handling the estate, especially when it is complicated and there are family members unable or unwilling to reach a consensus. This can potentially intensify the resentment they have toward each other. Many of these cases end up in mediation, which can be costly, and it can create even more bitterness when family members are forced by law to behave in a certain way. In these cases, the best course of action is to make sure everyone feels heard. If possible, gather the interested parties, pick a mutually respected facilitator, and set protocol for the meeting so that each person has the opportunity to speak. The goal is to break down the walls of anger and disappointment by providing everyone the opportunity to have a voice. Encourage questions and clarification and don't assume you know the whole story. In fact, being vulnerable and honest in these situations is truly the only way to make progress. If resources allow, it might even be in your family's best interest to engage a professional therapist or psychologist to help facilitate such a gathering. A neutral third-party voice might be the answer to all parties feeling comfortable sharing their real feelings, hopes, and fears.

In the aftermath of a death by suicide, survivors are forced to pick up the pieces at a time when they are in an immense amount of shock and pain. This often creates a feeling of resentment toward the person who has passed. In addition to absorbing the death, survivors are left with difficult questions; they may experience guilt for not having been successful in supporting their loved one – for not somehow preventing the suicide. And while I believe allowing time and space before you sort through the items is essential, that is not always possible. I once received a frantic phone call from a woman whose best friend, who had struggled with a lifetime of depression, had taken her own life, leaving her two teenage children shocked and confused. Their immediate reaction to the loss was to empty the entire house of their mother's belongings. In a fit of rage, they proceeded to throw all her personal belongings, along with pictures and any remembrances, out the front door and onto the front lawn. The woman who called me was inquiring about the best way to handle the situation. I shared with her that reasoning with the children at that moment probably wouldn't work – they had too much resentment toward their mother and fear for their future. I suggested that she pack up all the possessions from the front lawn and bring them to her home to store until the emotions settled down. In the end, the children were grateful to have remembrances of their mother.

Resentment caused by fear and disappointment surrounding a death or moving aging parents can be rectified, though. The key is permitting the involved parties time and space to regain their footing, allowing them to respond in a reasonable manner. As the anguish subsides, you can revisit the situation without preconceived outcomes.

Relationships with People

Relationships with people are complex and can change throughout a lifetime. We all know that we gain and lose friends as life goes on, but some life transitions can make this process a bit more abrupt or complicated. These moments of uncertainly about how to move forward beg the question, "Can relationships with people be considered possessions?" I think the answer is yes. And I think there are two main categories. There are your close friends, the ones you imagine would be there to support you through good times and bad, and there are friends who were closer to your loved one than they were to you. We build relationships with people at work, at school, within our neighborhoods, on vacations, through our religious affiliations, in social clubs, and during our activities. And while any of these relationships are a form of connection to a person's journey, they may not last forever. These relationships are part of our story, and following a death or life transition especially, the relationships may realign or dissolve, leaving a sense of emptiness. Some of those people you thought would always be present in your life now seem to be distant. The associations, memories, and experiences are part of remembrances and are forever connected to your heart, but not every friendship can last forever, especially following a traumatic experience, and that is okay.

In one of the entries in *Living with Loss, One Day at Time,* I address the void the situation causes with friendship.

Day 147
Where Have My Friends Gone?

They have gone back to their daily activities
and responsibilities. While you may feel as if
they have deserted you physically, they have
not in their hearts. Your friends have returned
to carpooling, vacationing, parenting, and their
normal routines. The difference is that your normal routine has changed, and you feel the void.

Remember, your friends don't know how you
are feeling on a daily basis, so be cautious
about taking it personally if you don't hear
from them as often. To help with the void, ask
them for help. As a friend of a griever, there
is nothing more fulfilling than being asked for
support. They are just a phone call, text, or
email away.

The most challenging relationships, those that are
not always straightforward, are those you may have
inherited through marriage or partnership. You have
been introduced to these people through your spouse or
significant other. What happens to these relationships
after a death? For example, when a widow sorts through
possessions, does that also include the relationships with
her spouse's family, college friends, or coworkers? Is it her
responsibility to redefine these relationships? Or should
she let them dissolve? Of course, if the friendship has
transcended the marriage and the relationship is strong

and solid, there is no reason to reconsider its place in your life. However, in many cases, relationships with in-laws or friends might become estranged or simply dissolve with mutual understanding. If you let go, is that the same as letting go of a personal possession?

The night Rod passed away, my mother-in-law looked me in the eyes, in heart-wrenching pain over the death of her youngest son, and asked me not to take her grandbaby away from her. At that moment, I knew she needed to be with our daughter forever because she represented a piece of her son. While continuing a connection with Rod's family wasn't always straightforward, I committed to fostering the relationships after Rod's death. Fortunately, this was a mutual desire, which made it much easier to actually execute over the years. With this goal of a continued relationship, all parties were committed to making time for each other.

While the previous example was related to family, what happens to those friendships that were really more acquaintances once the driving force of your loved one is gone? Not every relationship will feel the same; some may remain strong, while others dissolve or simply change. My advice is to savor what is, and don't feel guilty if you slowly part ways. You will always be connected through your mutual loss. What you decide to do with relationships will evolve over time, and if you are questioning what is best, place the people in your PONDER PILE and revisit them in the future.

New Marriage/New Partner After the Death of a Significant Other

For those of us who are fortunate to remarry or repartner, the recoupling and joining of personal items can be complicated, especially for the new partner and others who are unfamiliar with this type of loss. As I've discussed, in many cases, the new couple will continue to live in a house that was once occupied by the previous partner. The home is likely overflowing with items belonging to or shared by the deceased person, as it should be. At this point, many of the personal belongings such as clothing, toiletries, sports equipment, reading glasses, and the like will have been sorted, relocated, or stored; however, the shared items remain visible and practical for daily use.

In my case, when I remarried, Taner moved into the house I had shared with my deceased husband. Our home was overflowing with furniture, dishes, knickknacks, and household memories of my first marriage – including framed photographs. Taner was amenable to moving into "our" home, which was filled with love and sadness, and was the only home my daughter truly knew. When Taner moved in, he brought his personal possessions with him and merged them with ours, creating a warm and loving environment for the three of us to grow as a family. The photographs of Rod remained a fixture in our home for many reasons, although I did relocate them to less prominent places, giving space on the mantel and in our bedroom for photographs of my new family.

Those who have experienced a partner loss know the situation is not similar to a divorce, where there is often a desire to remove the partner's personal possessions along with the memories. With a death, we usually want the memories to be saved and cherished forever. Why would we have a SAVE PILE if we didn't want to see or touch our loved one forever?

I am often asked about living-arrangement solutions when repartnering. Is it best to create a new environment for you and your new partner, or should you adjust to the current arrangement? There is no doubt that creating a new life and home together is exciting and often the ideal scenario, but for most people, it is not feasible for numerous reasons. The concept of moving into, for example, a widow's home might be unfamiliar and unsettling to someone who has not experienced a loss. In fact, some people might believe the widow is "not over the loss yet" if there are personal possessions belonging to her deceased husband around the house. But in my opinion there is nothing to get over – the loss is part of who you are and your personal story.

Taner was often asked how he could move into someone else's house. Didn't he feel he needed his own space? Luckily for me, he didn't think twice about it, and he would always answer that he moved in with me and my daughter, not with Rod. In fact, he is still asked all the time what it is like for me to be married to two people. The simple answer is that he is not competing with Rod. Rod has his place in our family, and always will. And Taner has his place as well. And although Rod's possessions have dwindled over the years, he is still very much a part of our house.

There are many tricks to making the house feel different and fresh for your new partner so that you can both feel like you are starting anew, making the space feel cohesive and reflective of the next chapter you are beginning together.

- **Rearrange:** A simple fix that requires little more than a weekend's work is to rearrange your closets and some decor pieces. Just by rearranging the shelves in the closet, the frames on the mantel, some artwork on the walls, or even the dishes in the kitchen cabinets, you can make a home feel new and refreshed. As simple as it sounds, it really does the trick and can make your new partner feel like things have changed with their presence. If your clothes arc now hanging where your partner's once hung, no one has to worry about how your new partner is using the space compared with how your deceased partner did. It now feels totally different. This can also make your partner feel like they are not simply replacing something that once was different in your life.

- **Switch your routine:** Changing your routine slightly can also make you feel like you are in a new home, even if you haven't actually moved. Start with something simple like switching the positioning of your car in garage. The way you enter and leave your home can create a subtle psychological change that may shift how you experience your home, no matter how long you have lived there. And if you are now parked where your spouse once parked, you won't feel the emptiness of the space in the garage. Another option is to rearrange a home office. Even switching which wall a desk is facing can shift your perspective and allow for a mental transition to your new circumstances.

- **Redecorate:** When most couples move in together, one of the most exciting parts of the experience is learning about and blending your styles to make a home feel comfortable and reflective of how you identify as a couple. When one partner is moving into a space that was previously occupied by an equally import- ant person in your life, it can feel like their personality and style are not represented. If you aren't interested in investing in new furniture, simply repainting a few areas and purchasing some new decorative pillows can make a space feel transformed – and for much less money.

- **Create a shrine:** Creating a designated area in the house for displaying objects and memories of your previous partner can help alleviate uncomfortable feelings your new partner might have had if they'd been placed throughout the home. Especially if children are present, it would be nice to have a place to remember and recognize a readily accessible chapter from their past, and it also allows the new family to move forward together making new memories. This can be in the form of a wall of fame, a special bookcase, an office, or any other niche or corner in the house that seems appropriate, depending on the types of possessions you are wanting to display.

Having listened to many people who have remarried after a loss, I am always impressed and gratified by the amount of support and love a new partner can have in recognizing the significance of the deceased in the widower's life. And I am also equally touched by the amount of support and encouragement a family can provide in welcoming a new addition to the family, even if it was never expected. To me, the true testament of this is an unexpected gesture I received from Rod's parents when I remarried. In their dining room, they have a display of six wedding photographs, capturing each of their children on their wedding day. When I remarried, they added a seventh.

Shared Family Possessions

Family-accumulated possessions are those considered to be heirlooms passed down for generations; for example a parents' home, family-run business, or property such as land or a vacation home. Unfortunately, these categories are outside the scope of creating six piles and may require additional examination, consideration, and potential negotiation.

In a perfect world, parents with such assets would arrange their affairs in advance, prior to death or mental deterioration. Unfortunately, some families depend on the old-fashioned handshake and honor system, or they assume their children or siblings would never cheat or hurt one another.

If provisions have not been made in advance for a family-owned business, land, or house, legal action will have to be taken to determine the fairness of dividing the assets among family members. The situation can be further exacerbated if the family is not in agreement about whether to sell or keep the assets, or about the division of said assets. In the case of selling a property, do the other parties buy out those who want to keep it? What if they cannot afford the settlement price? Does one sibling deprive another from keeping the family house just because they can't afford it? In my line of business, I have observed families struggle with unsettled properties that wind up in litigation for years, causing stress for all parties – not to mention costing a great deal of money. While the parents' intention was to provide a special gift to their children, in reality, the children may well have differing opinions about what should happen to the property or business. In the case of a vacation home, what if two of the siblings use the property on a regular basis, but the third is not interested in the property at all? Who pays the taxes and upkeep? Is it fair to divide the cost by three? Clearly, the most logical approach would be to buy out the other sibling; however, that becomes difficult if the funds aren't available. Regrettably these situations will have to be resolved with legal counsel, so it is helpful to think of options to bring to the table that can help resolve the issue fairly for all involved.

If we look at the example of a family property that some want to keep and some want to sell, perhaps there are certain negotiations that can be agreed on that don't involve upfront money. Other ideas could include a potential trade of assets or a long-term financial contract.

Similar to family properties, if parents do not designate who should receive family heirlooms, how do the survivors divide or assign the items? Suppose the parents have three children and eight grandchildren – would it be appropriate for each person to receive a token gift, or should it be divided evenly among the children? How could one sibling determine what is right for another? Each sibling will have their own valid opinion of how the situation should be handled, but these may not be satisfying to everyone.

Whether a family is working through a loss or pending move, family dynamics are often difficult to understand. My preference is not to generalize when discussing family-shared possessions, as most families respect each other enough to find an amicable solution. For those cases that are not straightforward, I recommend outside support to resolve any discrepancies, with the goal of a favorable outcome for everyone.

STORING POSSESSIONS

Throughout this book, I have shared how important it is to maintain a connection to someone who has passed away, or if you are downsizing, creating a new home that maintains items that tell a person's story. Some of those items will enter your own home and be displayed permanently for you and others to view. The rest may be packed in boxes, stored for future sharing, rotated in or out, or saved for use in a future living arrangement. This is similar to revisiting our own closet from season to season; for example, it may take a few years to part ways with a sweater. Keep in mind that the key to storing items isn't to put the box in the back corner of a basement, never to be revisited. Instead, once you have your KEEP and PONDER PILES, set a timeline for yourself to return to the belongings you have stored, and when it's time, perhaps invite a friend or family member to help you while you reassess the items. Another person may ask questions triggering thoughts that help make a decision. In addition, you will be able to share stories of your past and your loved one.

For some, the obstacle isn't necessarily *what* to store, it's *where* to store it. Once when I was presenting at a conference, a woman shared that she had moved her husband's belongings into a storage unit that was costing her hundreds of dollars a month. While she knew the arrangement wasn't fiscally responsible, she couldn't bring herself to sort through the items but didn't want them in the house.

Sadly, she isn't the only one in this predicament. I have found when people are pressured by their family members to "clean out" their closets, they'll often move items to a storage unit that is their sanctuary to visit without being judged. If you can afford the extra monthly cost, that is an option for creating a memory room or shrine, but it's certainly not an ideal space for such a sacred connection. It is in situations like these where a team of trusted advisors and the six piles can help you tackle something that you have literally pushed out of sight.

The most common reason for storing items is for aging parents. When they downsize their homes, they ask their adult children to take things to store for them – things they aren't ready to part with that won't fit in their new home. Whether these items are clothing, old pictures, kitchen wares, or other personal items, I would recommend reboxing, resorting, and revisiting them on a regular basis. Most likely the boxes will contain belongings they will never use again such as cassette tapes, favorite articles of clothing that don't fit, and an assortment of old photos needing to be sorted and thinned. In most cases, the parents won't remember what's in the boxes, but that's not a reason to get rid of the items immediately. Instead, I recommend familiarizing yourself with what's in the boxes. Yes, certain things can be donated, and if your parents ask where they are, you can simply share that your local church or community center was asking for donations. As for the pictures, keep them. I suggest scanning the important ones and presenting a slide show or video to your parents on a holiday or special occasion.

There are also those rare times when you are asked to store things you don't want to, or you need to ask someone else to do it, someone who is perhaps not the ideal candidate. Recently, a woman shared a story with me about belongings of her stepdaughter's mother who had passed away sooner than expected. For legal and financial reasons, the daughter was forced to sell her mother's home immediately. She then asked her father and stepmother if she could store some boxes at their house until she felt ready to sort through them, or when she was in a living situation that would allow her to take them back. The stepmother was somewhat uncomfortable with this arrangement, but she agreed in order to help her stepdaughter. All parties were able to acknowledge that it might not be ideal, which went a long way toward eliminating any ill will or resentment down the line. Further, they were able to setting parameters and an estimated time frame, which also reassured the stepmother that this was not a permanent situation.

PERCEPTION THAT NO ONE WANTS ANYTHING

For many parents or other member of older generations who are cleaning out their homes and offering possessions to family and friends, there are sometimes hurt feelings when someone doesn't want something that once had great significance and purpose. I'll admit that I cringe when I hear "My kids don't want my stuff" from friends and clients. The truth is that they both do and don't. In reality, when they look at an offering of old furniture, clothes, shelves of books, and a pantry of kitchen items, they often see items that are either old, not stylish, too big, or simply not needed in their stage of life. But the reason I cringe is because I know there is a strong chance they want the stuff *not* offered to them rather than the stuff that *is*.

One big reason for this shift in thinking is that the lines between generations have been blurred by the continued evolution of electronics, internet access, online shopping, and even the slowing of the aging process with the advent of better medical and lifestyle practices. The generation gap is shrinking, and different age groups have become more similar in their daily activities, including choice of foods, exercise, social media, dress, and behaviors. If you think about it, we are driving the same cars, listening to the same music, traveling to the same foreign countries, reading the same books, watching the same television or streamed shows, shopping at the same clothing stores, using the same electronics (cell phones, tablets, laptops), drinking the same cocktails, eating in the same restaurants, and participating in the same sports. The days of the mindset that only adults golf, shop at nicer stores, or enjoy world cuisine are over. If our kids have the same access as their parents to new and exciting items, why would they want the old stuff?

For the giver, the feeling that "no one wants anything" is worthy of a conversation here. It stems from my desire to help you change your perception that your children don't want your personal possessions. Reconsidering the approach or reasoning behind an offering may influence or alter the opinion about the items being offered. And likewise, if you are able to ask why without getting defensive when you hear the answer, you can gain a better understanding of your children's needs and per-haps look at your own selections for them differently.

As I said earlier, sometimes children may believe you're giving them your junk, when in fact you're simply trying to help them build their life. A friend of mine recently told me a story about her neighbor insisting that she take her old lace-edged tablecloths and wouldn't take no for an answer. My friend kindly tried to explain that she simply didn't need them because she doesn't use tablecloths. With new furniture styles and different entertaining expectations, we no longer use tablecloths the way our parents did. She was grateful and honored by the offer, but simply had no use for tablecloths. Instead, she might have wanted the neighbor's collection of serving dishes and cookbooks, which could be genu-inely useful.

In another example, a friend shared a story of wanting to give her old couch to her son who lived two thousand miles away. Although a bit worn, the couch was expensive – nicer than anything he could afford. She was excited for him to have an "adult apartment" in spite of the cost of shipping a large piece of furniture that was ultimately too big. He knew he could purchase the right size couch from an online or local retail store at a compet-itive price and the item would be in stock and ready to be delivered in a few days. The mother felt slighted that her couch wasn't good enough; her motive was simply to help her son. This situation occurs every day with kids going off to college, moving into new apartments, and purchasing their first houses. They are desperately in need of furniture and housewares; however, there are often newer, faster, and cheaper resources that get them what they need with fewer logistical challenges.

What if the mother instead approached her son with an offer to assist that was more open-ended? Instead of offering just the couch, why not ask what he specifically needs to get settled in a new apartment. Most likely the son's list would include items of immediate need as well as items he would want later when he was more settled. I have often witnessed a change of behavior and interaction when approaching a situation this way. I was surprised by my friend's reaction. She knew that shipping the couch cross-country was more expensive than purchasing a new one, yet she was still offended. She thought about why she had such an adverse reaction to discarding a perfectly usable couch that she no longer wanted and determined that she wasn't comfortable "throwing away" something that cost so much and still had a useful life. I suggested that instead of sharing the couch with her son, she could be donating it to a charity or sell it in a consignment shop.

Changing your approach to focusing on the needs of the recipient rather than your own can help temper any potential offense. But perhaps there is a simpler resolution when wanting to gift a valuable possession. What if you're simply asking the wrong person? As I've mentioned throughout this book, it is important to think about your entire network when creating your SHARE PILE. In this case, the son was simply not the right person for that couch, but a local friend, neighbor, colleague, or charity might be. When you take the time to listen to why someone might not be interested in a particular possession, it might lead you straight to the right person.

Saying that no one wants anything is a general comment often used in jest, but it has a lot of underlying truths. If you ask your children what items they might be interested in keeping but receive no response, my suggestion is to make a list of ten items you would like your children to keep for the future. Think of the joy you'll feel if they accept at least one of the items. To avoid the feeling of rejection, add items to the list you are confident they would like to have. In the case of younger children or grandchildren who are not mature enough to make decisions, gather a few items and place them in a box to save for the future. Yes, this might be a gamble, but it's a risk worth taking.

Early in my career, a manager once told me that if all our challenges were straightforward, we would be bored and complacent. For the most part, sorting through your or a loved one's possessions will prove to be emotionally and possibly physically exhausting at times, but overall it will be a very rewarding and inspiring journey if you prepare well. As I've discussed, there will of course be times when you are faced with situations that are not as straightforward, but I suggest embracing the situation and trying your best to think creatively based on the resistance you are getting. The solution may not be to your liking, but I am confident a peaceful one is achievable. The decision-making process can create anxiety, but trying to eliminate the emotions and focus on the logic can help you find the best approach to resolving the challenges of possessions.

CHAPTER 5

BEING PREPARED, MANAGING YOUR POSSESSIONS, CREATING THE LIFESTYLE

Managing personal possessions is part of a lifestyle, an ongoing endeavor without a start or end date. The ultimate advice I can provide is to encourage you to create a lifestyle that includes being organized, removing clutter, having your affairs in order, and most importantly, not expecting your children or other family members to organize your belongings. By embracing this lifestyle, others won't have to worry about those matters when faced with an unexpected death or downsizing of your home; instead, your family will be able to embrace the loving memories created over the years.

My personal story clearly demonstrates that untimely deaths do occur; you can never be too prepared or start too early to get your affairs in order. Rod and I did make our will after our daughter was born and designated each other as beneficiaries on our life and medical insurance; however, we had not discussed final resting spots, a planned memorial, future parenting goals, or financial arrangements. Because of my personal experience and the challenges encountered by my clients, I am a fervent believer in being prepared in advance by embracing these otherwise challenging matters early on.

Many people perceive the notion of "getting your affairs in order" to be a task you do when you're older. While more people today can expect to live longer and healthier lives, there are still many people who suffer untimely deaths. And unfortunately, if there is not a plan in place, a family member will be responsible for tying up all the loose ends and sorting through all the personal belongings. For the person who is tasked with resolving the end-of-life responsibilities, it can be both overwhelming and uncomfortable when the person who passed was ill-prepared.

The lessons I learned from my own loss have changed my lifestyle habits; I am continuously sorting and thinning my closets and drawers and removing unwanted items or clothing I haven't worn in several years. But I am careful to save enough items that capture my life story, including mementos of my high school and college days, recognition of my athletic achievements, articles I've published, the launch of my first book, and other memorabilia. All of these items are neatly stored in a small box labeled "Rachel's personal possessions," which I revisit often. What happens to this box in the future is unknown, but for now, I enjoy reminiscing about my earlier years. And my family knows that the things I have chosen to save in this box are of particular significance to me.

This chapter is about being prepared for life's transitions and changes. It's about leading an organized life and acknowledging that saving unwanted and unneeded items can weigh you down. The majority of us tend to collect belongings in our thirties, forties, and fifties while we grow our family and furnish our home. As we begin to experience transitions such as growing older, downsizing our homes, and caring for aging parents, our priorities begin to shift away from accumulating assets. In our sixties and seventies, we instead have the desire to clear, disperse, and free ourselves of these items. Just as we learned earlier in this book how to sort and thin our possessions due to a death or downsizing a home, here you'll find tools, techniques, and reasons to create a lifestyle that prepares you for any life transition.

PREPARING – GETTING YOUR AFFAIRS IN ORDER, INCLUDING YOUR POSSESSIONS

We plan for many aspects of our livelihood, such as securing financial stability for ourselves and our children, insuring our home for unexpected disasters, engaging in preventive health care to ensure good health, and designating a person to be the custodian of our legal papers. Yet we often procrastinate getting our house and personal items in order should something unwanted actually happen. Many of us believe our affairs are in order after we have secured a financial advisor to guide us through estate and tax implications; an insurance specialist to protect our personal assets; a lawyer to aid in medical directives, wills, and trusts; and a funeral planner to help prepare for our final resting spot. But what about our personal possessions? Most of us do not have a specialist who can help reconcile our personal belongings – those possessions that tell our life's story and that we would like to be saved and shared with others.

There is no doubt that having end-of-life or what-if conversations are difficult, uncomfortable, and often awkward, as no one really wants to talk about preparing for aging or death. I like to tease my clients that if they have all their affairs in order, perhaps nothing sudden or unexpected will happen, since it's typically when we are ill-prepared that something unforeseen occurs. I have observed families tiptoe around the conversation, thinking the discussion is too personal or discourteous, and for some reason believing that if they talk about death they might actually die. A colleague of mine, whom I like to refer as the "death whisperer," has found a formula to encourage and support clients to be prepared by documenting their end-of-life wishes, including burial or cremation desires, what should be included in a eulogy, celebration of life wishes, and anything else that might help to create a less stressful arrangement for families. I have suggested to her that she should add a component of a "possessions specialist" to help prepare others with personal possessions. Typically, someone outside of the family would be the best person to support the process as they can ask probing questions without compromising a relationship. There is an inherent nonjudgmental trust not otherwise available that occurs when someone outside the family is available to support the organizing and sorting of personal belongings.

There is also a liberating feeling of not being responsible for items you've been saving over the years. While the concept of organizing and disposing of items before you die may seem morbid, many people, especially your family, will actually benefit from your actions. If you are more organized, your family is not left with the burden, and others will benefit from the items you donate now. As I shared earlier, creating a list of items you want to give to family members when you downsize or pass will likely prevent misunderstandings among family members (see p. 79). This approach provides you an opportunity to discuss your wishes with your family in advance, resolve any disagreements, and document the decisions you've made. To me, the biggest gift you can give yourself and your family is the opportunity to share stories associated with each heirloom, whether the item is your grandmother's candy dish, the glass doorknob from your grandfather's front door, or the gold-leafed clock that your great-grandfather had on his mantel. These are memories that should be passed along while you have the ability to share them.

BEING ORGANIZED, STAYING ON TOP OF YOUR POSSESSIONS

There can be a difference between being an organized person and how you manage, honor, and store your personal possessions. Being organized is a trait that you develop throughout your life, and it manifests itself by ensuring you can be on time, accomplish daily tasks, maintain a clean and tidy home, and follow up on email, phone calls, and other correspondence in a timely manner. Not everyone has a desire to be organized, however; for example, some people have no issue with stacking mail, newspapers, clothing, and other items that slowly grow into larger piles.

During my time working in the corporate world, I was amazed by how different coworkers organized their work spaces – some were neat and tidy while others had desks stacked with papers, old coffee cups, folders, office supplies, and other items of interest to them. I learned as I interacted with my coworkers that the condition of their office space quite possibly was a reflection of how they managed their home life, specifically their personal belongings. In other cases, I have observed people taking better care of their personal possessions than the space they live in. For example, one might keep their car and sports equipment in perfect condition, yet the sink can be full of dishes, laundry can be piling up, and children's toys may be scattered all over the family room. Being organized is truly in the eye of the beholder. Some people can live with piles since they know exactly what's in each one and where to find what they want when they need it.

Since we are talking here about being prepared and leaving less work for our family members after a life transition, we need to address our personal beliefs about what being organized really means and how that relates to our personal possessions. For me, organization is about creating a lifestyle of being prepared for changes by carefully and deliberately arranging belongings and reducing the quantity of items accumulated over the years. However, only you can define what being prepared and organized means for you. Think of a shoe thrown in a closet upside down that doesn't match its mate on the floor. Some might interpret that as a mess, while others would view the situation as just fine—the shoes are in the closet rather than by the front door or on the steps. In defining your perspective, first you have to clarify your vision of being prepared. Does that mean having all the rooms in your house organized? Or do you believe it is sufficient for the areas of your home that you live to be neat? For me, being prepared and organized is the ability to find what I am looking for when I need it, keeping my surroundings tidy, not collecting items I don't use, and neatly storing saved items for future generations in a closet, basement, attic, or garage.

Once you define your preferred level of preparation, you can create specific systems that work for you and your personal possessions. In defining your own system, I suggest you create a plan that incorporates your wants and needs to ensure success. For me, since I like my home orderly, my systems stem from my goal of being able to locate what I need when I need it. One might define this as a form of decluttering or extensive organizing; however, I look at it more as a lifestyle. Of course, like everything else, I might feel the creep of too many belongings in my storage area or the garage and will have to take the time to revisit these places. If you feel strongly about living with structure and a systematic approach to organizing, then it will happen. In the pages that follow, I'll share my tips and tricks. Remember: making the time and aligning your priorities are necessary to meet your goal. In most cases, you will achieve success if you create a lifestyle that suits your needs and is relatively easy to maintain.

My desire to maintain a "tight ship" stems from my upbringing, sharing space with college roommates, and creating a decluttered home for my family. However, sorting through Rod's belongings set in motion the additional desire that no one would ever have to organize my belongings after I pass. Of course, there will always be the need to follow the Magic of Six Piles; however, I consider that sorting and thinning, not organizing. I developed a lifestyle with my family that incorporates organizing and managing our personal possessions in our daily routines. When we first developed these approaches, we struggled to keep up, but over time we developed a rhythm. And now, we don't think of them as chores, nor do we feel this puts too much pressure or too many expectations on us. Managing our possessions is simply a part of our lifestyle, and we barely think twice about it. The ideas here are about incorporating daily actions that change the way you live, not just about adding dividers to drawers or redesigning a closet. For those who find getting started daunting, I would suggest finding a professional to help you. In my journeys, I have found an array of individuals who are available to help. In fact, with all the buzz surrounding declutter and organizing these days, teenagers have created organizing businesses to help people rearrange aspects of their homes. While not a true professional, this is a great way to manage costs and support neighbors and friends.

The following are a few tricks I have incorporated into my daily life. Feel free to use these, create your own, or seek assistance from friends or family:

- Design a place to "download" the items in your hands when you walk into your home. A specific place where you can recharge your electronics, hang your keys, place your purse or briefcase, and pile mail or other paperwork needing future attention. This is one way to keep from scattering items. And this will help you on the flip side, as you'll most likely need the same items as you walk out the door in the morning. In our home, we have a shelf in the pantry where we keep a charging station, there is a key holder hanging on the wall, and we have a shelf to place our purse or briefcase. For the most part, the pantry stays neat and tidy; however, there are times when we experience "the creep" and have to revisit to organize the items. Your area can also house anything that has not yet found its rightful place in your home. The goal is to not let items in the download area reach beyond the confines of the designated space.

- **Define your own game for staying on top of organizing clutter.** We have a motto in our house that when you leave for work or before you go to bed, you have to put away at least five things. The effort takes less than three minutes, and it truly works. Before I go to bed, I might place the tea cup in the dishwasher, pile the newspapers on the counter, take out the trash, clear the area of shoes, make sure there are no dirty clothes on the floor, or create a list of what I need to do before I leave the house the next day. While my five things vary from day to day, I must admit coming down the stairs in the morning to a more organized kitchen is one of the best ways for me to start a new day.

- **Create your own guidelines for going on vacation.** When I go on vacation, I prefer the house to be neat and tidy, which includes the laundry washed, the refrigerator cleared of perishables, items on the to-do list completed, and all papers cleared off the kitchen table. The reason is twofold: first, what if something happens to me, leaving someone else to deal with these things? And second, as I am pretty confident nothing will happen to me, coming home to a clean and orderly home after being away is truly delightful. When you walk in with your suitcase and souvenirs you are not overwhelmed with the feeling of reentry into reality or feel the need to clean up while preparing for returning to work or school. Before you leave, clear the kitchen counter, start the dishwasher, be sure the sink is empty, change the sheets and towels, tie up as many loose ends as possible, and clear your bedroom of clothes, shoes, and other items.

- **Maintain a digital plan.** Stay on top of your digital data by creating an organizational system to arrange and structure your personal data on your hard drive or the cloud. Once created, set a plan in motion for maintaining the stored files, which will keep your pictures, files, and saved data from becoming so overwhelming that you abandon your plan. And if you aren't comfortable with the ins and outs of digital life, ask for help from someone more savvy. Increasingly, I feel clients are more concerned about their electronic possessions than physical ones, mainly because they contain so much data. Just because it doesn't take up physical space doesn't mean that sorting and thinning the data would not take a great deal of time for a family member. As with your physical possessions, there are many ways to keep your data organized in files. Developing your own plan using a specific filing system and deleting old or unused data will keep it manageable. I do have a few tricks I use to keep my own data up to date, organized, and relevant. Since I travel often on airplanes with my computer, during the last twenty minutes of my flight, when I become restless before landing, I sort my photographs into files for easy access. I delete the pictures that are similar or are not favorites, crop the ones I keep, and organize groupings based on events. For some this may seem daunting, so you might want to choose a calm, quiet place with no distractions and plenty of time.

As I discussed, a crucial piece of organizing your digital life is your passwords (see p. 127). Create a list of all passwords – to access your devices, to log into bank accounts, for social media, and so forth – both for yourself and someone else should they need them in the event of your passing, and make sure you keep this list updated. There are many different platforms available to safely store log-on and password information using code words, protected applications, or your own system. Be sure to share the location of your passwords with someone you trust, in a safe, or with your other end-of-life affairs.

- Always have a donation bag handy. A simple but proven technique for assuring an article of clothing that doesn't fit well, is showing its age, or doesn't make you feel good about yourself needs to be donated and not returned to your closet. Why place something back on a hanger when you can fold it, place it in the bag, and donate all the contents once your bag is full?

- Develop a spring and fall closet cleaning plan. For those of us who live in a four-season climate, our goal is to sort, thin, and clean out our clothing closets twice a year. During the summer months, we place our winter clothing in the back of the closet moving our summer clothing to the front. This routine provides us an opportunity to clean the dust off the shelves that has accumulated over the prior six months and prevents the creeping of clothing items into other closets in the house. By touching each item at least twice a year, we are more likely to discard things that aren't favorites or that we don't use. And even if you live somewhere with a more consistent climate, designate two times a year to engage in the same process.

  In my home, we follow the same approach for our kitchen cabinets, drawers, and pantry. We dust the items, vacuum the crumbs from the drawers, and remove duplicates of items that we don't use. I imagine we all have a few too many coffee cups and water bottles that can be donated.

There are great rewards to maintaining an organized lifestyle. For starters, you'll be able to live more freely with less weight and bulk holding you down. But just as with all the concepts I discuss, I recommend that you find the right balance for you. Even if you feel that your needs differ, at some point what to do with your possessions will need to be addressed. The notion of leaving the items for someone else to be responsible for is difficult for the recipient. While these ideas may help ready your home for downsizing or your passing, it is really so much more – they are a way of life, so I recommend you embrace them.

SIMPLIFY YOUR LIFE AND YOUR POSSESSIONS

By simplifying your life and your possessions you can maintain tidiness with less time and effort, your home and surroundings will look and feel better, you will become more efficient since you won't be searching for items, and you can actually create more time for yourself each day. By reorganizing your possessions and allowing immediate access to everything you need, you will shave minutes off your routine each morning and even more in the evening as you prepare for the next day.

Consider your clothes closet. Can you find and easily access the outfit you're looking for in an overcrowded closet? Since it's nearly impossible to wear all the items you have hanging there, why not eliminate those pieces that your never or rarely wear. We have a tendency to wear our favorite outfits anyway, so having fewer items allows you to better access what you love. By rightsizing the amount of clothing and footwear you own, you can actually enjoy what you do have and prevent contention in your own closet. For example, will you really wear twenty pairs of boots in one season? It's unlikely, yet many of us hold on to all our shoes despite never wearing them. Simplify your shoe collection by eliminating the ones that are uncomfortable, those that are a bit worn out, or the ones you have yet to actually wear. You may have to accept the fact you made a bad purchase and donate the pair for someone else to enjoy. As you reduce the number of shoes, your closet is more manageable, you can make quicker decisions, and you're wearing your favorite things.

Similar to offering tricks on how to organize your possessions, here are a few ideas to manage your possessions:

- **Make sure everything has its own place**. What I have found to be essential in simplifying my lifestyle is to know everything has its own designated space. Unavoidably, during the day items are removed from drawers, closets, and purses when being used. As the day progresses, we tend to pull out more items than we put away. So when it's time to straighten up, place each item back in its own designated place – in a closet, kitchen cabinet, or the garage. Using this approach, the items won't accumulate on the counter, floor, or in a corner. By assigning a place for each possession, the idea of putting away five items each morning and each evening is feasible, which allows for a simplified home.

- **Manage your to-do list differently**. Once a month (sometimes more often) I like to check off items on my to-do list in the order they have been written. Many of us who use to-do lists have a tendency to skip items that are more complex, require additional effort, or are of less interest. Instead of accomplishing that particular task, we forward the task to the next day or skip it altogether. In simplifying your list, you open the door to being successful with other tasks.

- **Limit the quantity of clothes hangers you have in your house**. Years ago, our family incorporated a closet rule stating that purchasing additional hangers is off-limits. Even though hangers are fairly inexpensive, the goal was that when you purchased a new shirt, you'd have to get rid of one. When you purchased a new pair of shoes, an old pair should be added to the donation bag. Every time a new purchase came into the house, something had to go. As an example of how we allow items to accumulate, I have seen runners save twenty-five or more pairs of running shoes as they switch to new ones frequently to prevent injury. Although a runner may not want to run in the shoes anymore, there is so much life left in them. Why not donate them, allowing someone else to use them and thereby simplifying your clutter?

- **Learn to travel lighter**. Airlines are forcing us to change the way we travel, and maybe that's a good thing. A seasoned traveler has the ability to pack for any length of a trip in a carry-on bag or reasonably sized checked bag. With the cost of checked baggage and the use of shared rides, towing excessive amounts of luggage to your final destination has become a thing of the past. A new outlook on travel could include wrinkle free, re-wearable, and mix-or-match clothing. The approach to travel is no different from simplifying your closet with items that are more practical, that you love, and that make you feel good. In addition to traveling lighter and more efficiently, I am loyal to my feet, therefore I choose shoes for travel based on city walking, business attire, or if I am attending a special event and limit the pairs of shoes in my suitcase to free up space for other needs.

- **Use electronic data to your advantage**. If you haven't already, begin paying your bills electronically to simplify your home office, receive your financial statements digitally, and reference your user manuals via the internet. By adopting those three modest changes, you will eliminate the need for paper folders, filing cabinets, and storage in your home office.

Afterword

Throughout this book, I've discussed the ideas of being prepared, managing your possessions, and creating a lifestyle, with the objective of planting seeds to help you manage your and your loved one's personal possessions. The pages are filled with ideas and thoughts to help you determine what works best for you and your family. You can embrace them completely, you can use them as a guide – experimenting with what works best for you – or something in between. Truly, there is no beginning or end, no right or wrong, no perfect or erroneous approach. Take what you have found here, and make it your own.

In Chapters 1 through 4, I've mapped out at length suggestions for sorting, thinning, and reassigning items, usually following a loss or when downsizing family members into a smaller living arrangement. The message in Chapter 5 is to then take the approaches, ideas, and lessons learned to create a lifestyle that helps you prepare and simplify for a life transition – an approach that streamlines your day-to-day life as well. I feel strongly that leaving the responsibility for your children, friends, or other family members to make decisions on your behalf can be difficult and unfair. By adopting routines, maintaining a pride in organizing, and getting your affairs in order, you will master the notion of being prepared.

While writing *Finding Peace, One Piece at a Time*, I found myself sharing different aspects of my thoughts and ideas with friends and family members. What was universally and profoundly present was that we all view the idea of possessions differently and therefore have approached losses and downsizing in different ways. Those who have not experienced a loss have a tendency to question why I would write a book on possessions, while others repeatedly shared they wished I had written this earlier. As I shared in the beginning, my relationship and understanding of possessions changed dramatically when Rod passed away.

Finding Peace, One Piece at a Time illustrates the importance of possessions and our relationship to them. And while these relationships may change over time, in the end, our personal belongings tell a story of our life, whether they have been handed down from generation to generation or collected throughout our own lifetime.

About the Author

No one knows better
how to embrace life's
challenges than Rachel
herself. After losing her
husband unexpectedly
at thirty-one years old,
she was left to raise
their young daughter
and say goodbye to the
life dreams they were
just starting to realize
together. Her experience
of sorting, thinning, and
redistributing his personal possessions over the years has
guided her to capture "his story" so it can continue to be
shared with current and future generations.

As a newly solo mother working full time in corporate
management, Rachel learned quickly that overcoming
life's most unpleasant realities requires a level of practicality and rational thinking that is hard to utilize when
blinded by overwhelming emotion. Since losing her
husband, Rachel has altered her career course to help
fellow grievers find a way through their pain and continue
to live a meaningful and happy life. She now presents
nationally, impressing audiences and readers with her
down-to-earth and relevant insights. Her goal is always

to help individuals reach their potential by embracing and learning from all of life's complexities. She is sure to inspire and persuade you to be self-aware, take action, and continue to thrive.

In her bestselling book, *Living with Loss, One Day at a Time*, Rachel offers daily encouragement to individuals and families who have lost a loved one or is experiencing any adversity. The 365 daily thought-provoking ideas provide hope, optimism, introspection, and self-discovery. Reflecting on her own return to work following the death of her husband, she also developed and published material about how to support grief and loss in the workplace. Her management handbook, *Grief in the Workplace: A Comprehensive Guide for Being Prepared*, has a wide circulation in corporations across the country.

Rachel remarried and now lives an active lifestyle in Colorado with her husband, Taner. When she is not writing or presenting, you can find her skiing, trail running, hiking, and spending as much time outside in the Rocky Mountains as possible.

READER REVIEWS

As a financial advisor, I so often see the struggle and stress that comes before a parent passes: "How can I convince my parents that all that stuff needs a place when they are gone? How will we get through it all?". And then after a loved one passes: "This has taken over my life," or "I can't do this." And I too have that same dilemma – my own father is a hoarder and we can see the end of his life in the not too distant future. I can help with the money part. That's within my skill set. But I can't help with the "stuff." Rachel can, though. *Finding Peace, One Piece at a Time* helps us wrap our arms around the emotional and the physical difficulties that we face when we are left with the belongings of those we love, and guides us through it all at our own pace. Thank you for helping me provide the answers to the questions I couldn't answer before.

Ora DeMorrow,
Senior Financial Advisor, Vice President, Merrill Lynch

This book tackles the topic of choosing what to do with a loved one's possessions in a sensitive way, offering tips and practical advice. This is a must-read for anyone who has ever had a loss. I wish I had read this book after my teenage brother died, as we impulsively gave away all his possessions, and later had regrets. Rachel delivers her promise, as you really will find peace one piece at a time, as you sort through, thin out, and redistribute the valued possessions that hold so many cherished memories for you.

Dr. Gloria Horsley, President and Founder of Open to Hope

Dr. Heidi Horsley, Dr. Heidi Horsley Psychological Services, LLC, Executive Director, Open to Hope Foundation

What do you do when "stuff" becomes "keepsakes?" When a loved one dies, material things suddenly become reminders of our loved one and special treasures. In her book, *Finding Peace, One Piece at a Time*, Rachel Kodanaz shares her personal experience as she guides readers lovingly through the sorting process of our loved one's material possessions. A truly helpful and practical book for sorting through "stuff" and grief.

Janet Roberts, Executive Director, Centering Corporation, and Editor, *Grief Digest Magazine*

The practical advice and gentle guidance available in *Finding Peace, One Piece at a Time* can provide hope to those who are facing the reality of what to do after a death. This book serves as a resource that can benefit anyone who has experienced a loss, has aging parents, or contemplated how to be more thoughtful about what "things" are meaningful and how to communicate that to those we love now and after we are gone. As a funeral director for more than twenty years I can confidently recommend this book to client families. I can see someone picking it up and going right to the topic that is most relevant at the time, and picking it back up to address one chapter at a time, in whatever time works for the individual.

Shannon R. Martin, Funeral Home Manager, Olinger Crown Hill Mortuary and Cemetery (Dignity Memorial)

In *Finding Peace, One Piece at a Time*, Rachel brings her compassionate, experienced, and honest insight to the difficult problem of what to do with the possessions of a loved one who has passed on. *Finding Peace* provides badly needed help for those left with an often-daunting task of sorting through possessions and the resulting, sometimes difficult emotions. With a step-by-step process that acknowledges the complexities of grief, possessions, memories, and history, Rachel guides those who need to sort, store, and dispose of possessions in a practical, compassionate, and frank manner.

Sara Wilson, Executive Director, Feminine Power MBA, PCC

Rachel is a compassionate coach who breaks down the seemingly insurmountable task of organizing one's life into a game plan for success. She speaks from the heart with practical, manageable tips and suggestions to help readers overcome the obstacles on their path to peace. If we could all effectively deal with the "stuff" in our lives according to this guidebook, there would be much less stress and much more harmony in the world.

Cindy Bramble, TAPS Institute for Hope and Healing®

Rachel Kodanaz has written an easy-to-read, step-by-step manual for managing the items in our lives that hold both meaning and memory. This practical little handbook will assist you in making your way through the often-difficult task of repurposing and decluttering during and after a variety of life transitions. Grab this book, gather your team, and begin the journey of peaceful discovery using Rachel's relevant process.

Michele Neff Hernandez, President and Founder,
Soaring Spirits International

Rachel Kodanaz's personal experience of grief has left her with profound wisdom about how to cope with this most painful, but most human, aspect of life. *Finding Peace, One Piece at a Time* is an essential companion for your journey through your loved one's personal belongings. Rachel has crafted a poignant, practical, and compassionate guide on how to approach and carry out sorting through, thinning out, and repurposing your loved one's possessions in a style that is personal to you.

Kristi Shahnazarian, Senior Account Consultant,
Trion Group, a Marsh & McLennan Agency LLC